God Won

HOW GOD USED PRAYER JOURNALING TO TEAR DOWN MY WALLS

SHERYL CRANE

Dear Kristen,

May you encounter Christ daily and enjoy true fellowship with the all-powerful, storm-calming, wall-demolishing King of kings and Lord of lords.

Seek Him with your whole ♡, and He will be found.

– Jeremiah 29:13

Sheryl Crane

S. Crane

i

GOD WON
HOW GOD USED PRAYER JOURNALING
TO TEAR DOWN MY WALLS
Published by GW Christian Publications, L.L.C.
gwchristianpublishing@gmail.com

Unless otherwise noted, all scripture is taken from the HOLY BIBLE, NEW INTERNATIONAL VERSION. Copyright© 1973, 1978, 1984 International Bible Study. Used by permission of Zondervan Bible Publishers.

ISBN: 979-8-9861114-0-7

The Team: William Bode, Rodney Crane, David Hansen, Sara Hansen, Delia King, Dorothy Mercer, Suzanna Monard

Cover Design: Matt and Adrian Petree

Printed in the United States of America

First Edition 2022

Dedication

This book is dedicated to William and Lyssa Bode and all my Christian Belgian friends I was blessed to meet in 2019 on my first trip to their country. At that time, I witnessed William and Lyssa working unceasingly and with great faith as they encouraged and modeled for Christians in Belgium (and beyond) to walk and pray in the Spirit of Christ and spread the gospel to the about 98% Belgians who don't know Jesus yet. I know they continue to do this. When purchasing this book, you have helped support their mission and future mission trips. I hope you pray with me now and continue to support the Belgians, as well as many others in Western Europe, in your prayers. Maybe one day you will be inspired to travel to Belgium and help them out also. William and Lyssa are always encouraging fellow Christians to visit.

Sheryl

Dear God,

We pray that You will richly bless William and Lyssa Bode and their fellow Christians in Belgium as they put their trust and confidence in You. May You continue to lead and guide them, and may they produce much fruit for You.

In Jesus' Name we pray, Amen.

Contents

Introduction

I was sitting at my computer after teaching my volunteer computer class at Brockway Christian Academy. I had just sent the students back to their main learning center. Scanning through my emails for a return message from 12Stone Church, I was a little frustrated because there was no message yet. I had been directed to send questions there about Kevin Meyers' book called Grown-up Faith[1]. You see, I had just returned from a mission trip to Belgium a few weeks earlier. God had placed it on my heart that the people there needed encouragement to grow in their faith and there aren't very many Christian books in Dutch or French for them when compared to the abundance of Christian literature in America.

At that time, I was reading Grown-Up Faith[2] by Meyers, and I thought, "This is a great book! They should be able to have the opportunity to read it in their own language." I emailed Meyer's church. The heavy sigh I gave when I saw there was no reply within 24 hours shows that God is not through working within me yet.

Then, this strange thought came to me. "Why don't *you* write a book? You could write a book for people who want to grow in their relationship with the Lord. You can have it translated into Dutch and French for the Belgians." Meyers says that when you hear a little voice in your head that challenges you to do something that is not contradictory to what the Bible says or with God's character and principles, then it's probably a God-prompt. Even if the idea may seem so far-fetched, crazy and some might dare say impossible, you better move forward.[2] Hence, I closed up my computer, and in a daze, I headed down the stairs, out through the learning center, and down the hallway to the office. Pastor Rachel, the school's secretary, greeted me with her usual smile. I said, "I think God just asked me to write a book!"

"Wow!" Pastor Rachel exclaimed.

"I know!" I replied with tears streaming down my face.

While driving home, I was thinking that maybe He wants me to write a how-to book on how I do prayer journaling. I was thinking of a short, simple book. "Yes, that's doable," I thought. On my way through town, I stopped and talked to Greg Hetherington, the owner of Books in Back Bookstore. I had just met him a couple of days before and found out that he takes people's book ideas and formats them so they are ready to be published into a book. I thought that maybe he could help me out. When I got home, I texted William and Lyssa Bode, the missionaries who I stayed with and helped in Belgium, the exciting news. William replied, "Sheryl, write me a proposed table of contents, an introduction, and your first chapter. Maybe we can publish it."

"Wow! Not a short, simple book, huh, God?" I prayed. "You want me to write a chapter book? Ok, but You're going to have to give me the ideas."

After I finished my lunch, I thought I had better start preparing for the lesson I was going to help teach for Children's Worship that Sunday at my church, Lakeview Community Church (LCC). LCC is a Wesleyan church located in an old furniture store at the main intersection in rural Lakeview, Michigan.

As I was reading through the material, I could see the connections it made to my own life. I quickly started writing down the ideas as they seemed to pour from my pen. A few hours later, I texted back William. "God works quickly," William said when I told him I had a title, an introduction, and a table of contents. Oh, I knew it may change many times over by the time I was finished, but it was a start. Because you see, I have learned it is just best not to put off what God places on my heart to do. However, things were not always this way for me. God had a lot of walls to tear down first.

Let me explain a little of what I mean by walls. The lesson my friend Lori and I were

4

going to teach that Sunday was from Joshua 5
and 6 about Joshua fighting the battle of Jericho
and how God collapsed the walls of Jericho. To
me this story really shows how when we trust
God and do what He says to do, even though we
may not understand it, He will come through
with what He promised. The creators of this
lesson used this story to show how God can give
us a big victory by knocking down any walls we
may have made to keep Him away from us.
These walls, I believe, are the lies Satan tells us
and we believe. As I read through the lesson, I
thought of the walls God has had to work at
tearing down to get me to where I am today: the
"I don't matter" wall, the "I'm not good enough"
wall, and the "I need to have control" wall.
When I compared what I thought the story of
Joshua fighting the battle of Jericho was about
and what the creator of the lesson's focus was, I
see how they both come down to a matter of
trust. Do I trust God enough to let Him break
down my walls and let Him come in? "Yes!" I
thought. "This is what my story is all about. This

is what I think God wants me to tell. He wants me to give my testimony."

I invite you to come with me on a journey to see how God used prayer journaling as a way to knock down my walls and possibly, by reading this book, you will be encouraged to let God tear down any walls you have built up, maybe even the "I'm too busy" wall.

You will notice that I call God "Daddy." To me, God is my loving Father and I am His child. I feel so privileged to have an intimate relationship with Him, a Father worthy of my total respect. That's why I call Him Daddy.[4]

You will also notice that in this book, my prayers and prayer journal entries are in a different font.

1

As We Seek Your Face

Ecclesiastes 3:11 states that God has "set eternity in the human heart."

Dear Daddy,

Thank you for giving us forever! This joy that I've found in You cannot be taken away by the world because the world didn't give it to me. My spirit praises you with the group, I Am They, as we sing "We Are Yours". – Hallelujah!! Thank you for placing eternity in our hearts. Because of this, we are aware that there is something more to this life than what we can see in the here and now. This longing You give us helps us to know that we will never be fulfilled, or satisfied, with what this world has to offer. It causes us to seek You. May we seek You and Your kingdom first every day!

William Bode, a missionary in Belgium whom I served with in 2019, said to me one time that he thinks that what I do when I'm prayer journaling is like meditating. Hence, as I was writing this book, I looked up Christian meditation online, and I came across this cool article called, "10 Things You Should Know about Christian Meditation" by Sam Storm that describes pretty much what I do.[1] You can google search this article by typing in "Sam Storm Christian Meditation" to find it. Go to this website and see for yourself.

I explained how I journal for my prayer journal workshop:

- Write down and think about the You Version Bible app daily verse.

- Think and write about one of these things:
  - What God is saying to me about who He is
  - How He is asking me to live my life
  - How I can apply the verse or change it into a prayer
  - What the verse reminds me of, like a song or an experience
  - Any questions I have about the verse, like the meaning of a word or the verse itself, or look at the whole chapter to get it in context
- I may look online at Christian websites and compare their answers with one another and with the Bible. God calls us to be alert.[2] So I try to be cautious when reading, viewing, or listening to anything other than the Bible.

- Sometimes I pick a devotional topic in the app or in a book. Then, I read through it, take notes, summarize the important parts, and record my own thoughts or questions I may have.

- I take sermon notes and add my own thinking or application and perhaps discuss these in my small group.

- I write interesting God conversations I've had with people.

- I write about the times when I've seen God at work in my life.

- I spill my heart out to God and confess my sins. I ask for and thank Him for forgiveness, grace, and mercy. I cast all my cares on Him. I thank Him for His promises and the hope they give me. I thank Him for being able to come into His Holy presence by the blood of His precious Son.

How is it possible for two people who have never met to come up with pretty much the exact same way that drew them closer to God?

How is it that I, who have never studied what Christian meditation is, am doing exactly that? I believe it to be the work of the Holy Spirit. I believe it is because people have been praying for me, and because of that, God softened my heart so I was able to come to Him with a humble heart and fall down at His feet. I would come to realize how sovereign and Holy He is. I would seek His face. I would want Him to draw me close, closer to Him. I would desire to worship and obey Him, knowing that I truly needed Him to help me. He did. And He still does.

As a matter of fact, while working on revisions of this book, I have come to find even more ways that have helped me to grow in my relationship with God. Jill, a friend I met on a mission trip, led me to download the Blue Letter Bible app on my phone. You can study versions of the Bible side by side. What I like most is that you can read the commentaries from different pastors for every verse. Suzanna, a friend of William, who is translating this book into Dutch, also discovered that you can listen to these sermons by going to the audio/video section. That's very helpful for when you're taking your dog for a walk or when you're driving in your car and don't want to listen to the radio. Later, I like to write in my journal anything that really stuck out to me. The app also has a Bible dictionary, which is a great tool for getting a deeper understanding of the meaning of words. I've also come to see the value of going through the whole Bible. I'm sure there are many ways to do this, but one day, I stumbled across Dr. Vernon McGee's podcasts and have been "aboard the Bible Bus" since then. Now I just google search by typing the name of the book I'm studying and then "thru the Bible series with Dr. Vernon McGee." I first like to read the Bible passage myself before I listen to the podcast. This way I can compare my own insights, which I have written down in my prayer journal, with those of Dr. Vernon McGee while listening to his podcast.

No, I do not think you have to keep a prayer journal to have a close relationship with God. I know they did not have them in Noah's day or even in Abraham's. I also believe there are many people who do not have the means to buy them who are still close to God's own heart. I know too that my Aunt who was mentally impaired could not possibly keep a journal. However, I know she loved Jesus, and I know she loved others. Anytime anyone came to see her she would exclaim, "My pal!"

Prayer journaling is not just the latest Christian fad either, like some people think of bullet journaling. I think that since it appears that King David kept something similar to a prayer journal, which we refer to as the book of Psalms, people have been writing down their prayers as early as five centuries before Christ. Actually, what I've found is using the written prayers of David and of Paul the Apostle helps me to better express myself to God and how to turn my heart to the truth amidst my own confusion. They are an example to me of how to repent of the sin in my life and how to pray when I've felt depressed or discouraged in my faith. They have also taught me how to praise the Lord and how to pray for fellow believers, others and myself. I have often found myself turning to the written prayer of Jesus in Matthew 6 to guide me on how to pray.

No, I do not write down all my prayers. From watching our Youth Pastor Ben Stout, Jr. at Youth Group and listening to William at prayer meetings, I have also seen how important spontaneous prayer is. Often times as Christians, we will tell someone, "I'll pray for you." Then, if you are like me, sadly we forget. Because of this, I learned that when someone is sharing a concern or a joy with me, why not pray with them right then and there. What matters most, whether written or not, is that your prayers come from your heart.

Prayer is very powerful! I can testify to all the prayers that I have seen being answered. What really matters, and I believe is essential to

Christian living, is coming to the Lord with a humble heart and meditating on Him day and night, especially on His Holy Word, the Bible. Scripture backs this up: Joshua 1:8, Psalm 1:1-2, Psalm 119: 15, 23, 48, 97, 99, 103, 148. I have found that writing prayers down enables me to slow down and reflect on what God is doing or has done.

There are many spiritual disciplines: Bible Study, Prayer and Meditation, Journaling, Fellowship, Worship, Solitude, Stewardship and Service (Ministry), and Fasting. The way in which I journal incorporates a few of these. As with any spiritual discipline, you need to be cautious not to make it the end itself, as the religious leaders in Jesus' day did. Rather, prayer journaling should be a means to the end: the end being drawing near to the heart of God.

One time I missed a day, and this is what I entered the next morning:

Dear Daddy,

AS WE SEEK YOUR FACE

I missed writing in my journal yesterday, but I had a very nice devotional time with Rod (my husband). I know it is not necessary for my salvation to keep a journal, but it sure does help me to stop, listen and reflect on what You have to say to me.

Someone in one of my prayer journaling workshops commented, "It takes a lot of discipline to do that."

I had to really stop and think about it before I answered, "I suppose so." It does not feel like discipline to me though. At first, it did, but now it is more of a compulsion. It is kind of like eating for me. I just have to do it. In order for me to get my half-hour of exercise in daily, I have to be disciplined. I do it so I do not have sore joints and get stronger bones, but I have to really talk myself into it. It's not that way for me to be in God's presence journaling. I delight in it. I feel awed that the creator of everything would want to spend time with me. I love to let

16

Him know that I know He's there for me, and He's working all things out for my good.[3]

Sometimes I do not even realize I've been praying for something, but He has a way of showing me that He is there and He knows my every thought and desire as I seek to do His will. Here are just a couple of examples of how I have seen this:

When I was getting ready for a mission trip to Honduras, I had to limit the amount of clothing I brought due to the other materials we were taking to leave behind. I thought it would be nice to have a white skirt, because it could go with almost any colorful top I was taking with me to leave behind. I had this image in my mind of exactly the kind of white skirt I wanted: puffy, frilly, down-right girly. Every garage sale I went to that spring, I looked for such a skirt. I found a two-dollar skirt that was miraculously my size, and it was white, but it was too business-like. The search continued. It was just a few weeks before my trip, and I still had not found the skirt I desired. "Maybe I should try J.C. Penney," I thought. "They have nice clothes." I wandered in the store searching for the skirts. I came to one that looked just like what I had imagined. I tried it on. It was perfect! Then, I looked at the price. "Sixty dollars for a skirt!" I exclaimed to my husband, Rod, who was patiently shopping with me. "No way!" Then we headed straight for the door and walked right out of the store.

Disappointed, I got in the car, and we drove toward home. On the way, I thought maybe we should try Goodwill, a secondhand store, which was on our way. Once inside, I headed straight for the rack of skirts and looked for the ones in my size. It was not long before I spotted the white skirt that I had been looking for all along. Three dollars, YES! "Thank You, Lord!" I exclaimed. I felt like a grateful, much-loved child getting just what she wanted from her daddy. Later, I wrote in my journal:

Dear Daddy,

Great is thy faithfulness, Lord, unto me . . . all I have ever needed You have provided! Thank You for giving me the skirt for Honduras that I was looking for! If it be Your will, I will leave it behind. (I ended up not leaving it behind but decided to take it back with me for future mission trips. It would come in handy to go with any shirt I picked out to leave behind again.)

Often God sends me verses as reminders that He is with me as I seek to do His will. They are repeats of verses He gave me during my devotions or preparations for kingdom work. They bring a chuckle and a smile to my heart. One of these occurrences happened on a Sunday evening at the weekly youth group gathering. Here's what I wrote that night:

Dear Daddy,

That was cool, Lord, with Pastor
Ben repeating the verse You gave me in the
morning – You will give me everything I
need to do Your will to bring You glory![4]

The morning of my first prayer
journaling workshops, God gave me Proverbs
27:17 as the daily verse, which is the verse I used
to show people why I choose to share how I do
my prayer journaling. I chuckled as I wrote back
to Him:

Dear Lord,

You have such a way to affirm
who You are. I hear You say, "Yes, my
child, I did call you to Belgium. Keep
listening. Keep listening."

You should have heard the expressions
of the people during my workshop when we
were finishing up and some were downloading
the YouVersion Bible app onto their phones
(Yes, they can get it in Dutch! How cool is that!).

"Look! It's the same verse!" they gleefully exclaimed.

When you really stop to consider how awesome God truly is and how much He faithfully cares about us, how can you not want to spend time with him? How can you ignore his text messages? How can you not call Him back when He says, "Hey honey, call me back when you're not so busy."? How can you not put Him first? What walls are holding you back? He wants a relationship with you, just as He wants one with me. Your prayers to Him from a humble heart are like sweet perfume.[5] It pleases Him when we come to Him. I don't know about you, but there is nothing I want more than to please my Heavenly Father.

Dear Daddy,

I pray like the songwriter of "As We Seek Your Face", Dave Bilbrough, that Jesus would draw us closer to Him. I pray that we may all come before You

AS WE SEEK YOUR FACE

with open, humble hearts ready to worship and obey.

2

Who Am I?

"When I consider Your heavens, the work of Your fingers, the moon and the stars, which You have set in place, what is mankind that You are mindful of them, human beings that You care for them?" (Psalm 8:3-4)

"Your love, LORD, reaches to the heavens, Your faithfulness to the skies. Your righteousness is like the highest mountains, Your justice like the great deep. You, Lord, preserve both people and animals. How priceless is Your unfailing love, O God! People take refuge in the shadow of Your wings. They feast on the abundance of Your house; You give them drink from Your river of delights. For with You is the fountain of life; in Your light we see light. Continue Your love to those who know You,

Your righteousness to the upright in heart. May the foot of the proud not come against me, nor the hand of the wicked drive me away." (Psalm 36:5-11)

Dear Daddy,

I think of your love for us as constant and unchanging. My spirit sings along with Ryan Stevenson in "No Matter What." But I cannot understand why Your Word says in Malachi 1:2-3, "Yet I have loved Jacob, but Esau I have hated." Why doesn't it say, "I hate what Esau did-selling His birthright for a bowl of soup."? Of course, that's assuming why You hated Him. But Paul reminds me in Romans 9:14-26, who am I to question God? The potter, God Almighty, has the right to make out of the same lump of clay some pottery (people) for special purposes and some for common use. You, Lord, have the

24

right to do with people as You see fit. You have the right to have mercy on whom You have mercy and compassion on whom You have compassion.

I learned from C.H. Spurgeon in a sermon titled "Jacob and Esau"[1] that You were infinitely gracious – that is why You loved Jacob. Not because of what Jacob did. You chose Jacob in Your sovereign exemption of the consequences of his sins by giving Jacob mercy, or free grace. You hated Esau because Esau deserved it as a result of his own evil works. That is justice.

You remind us not to despise our birthright and sell it for that miserable mess of pottage – the pleasures of the world! You promise us that if we believe on the Lord Jesus Christ, we shall be saved.

WHO AM I?

I am a sinner, saved by grace! I
deserve the eternal fires of hell. Praise
be to You, God, for Your free grace – I
don't deserve it – I can't earn it – You did
it all for me. To You be the glory!

I'm assuming that by taking the time to read this book, you are interested in growing in your faith and relationship with the Lord. If you haven't already gotten a journal, you may want to pick one up now and begin prayer journaling by reflecting upon some of the thoughts and questions you have while reading this book. You could even just write in this book or take notes on your phone. If you take notes on your phone, you could print your notes off later, if you want to keep them in a book.

In this chapter we are discussing several questions that God has led me to wonder about in my own spiritual journey. He may be asking you to consider these questions also as you draw

26

nearer to Him. So, please, slow down your reading and take time to prayerfully reflect upon and consider your answers to these questions. This chapter is not intended as a quick read through, but a time to get into the habit of getting honest with God about your thinking and feelings and asking Him to guide you with the help of the Holy Spirit and through reflecting upon Scripture as He leads you on a closer walk with Him.

What stage would you think you consider yourself to be in if your walk with God could be described in the following stages: dead, infant, child, young adult, parent?

During one of my prayer journaling workshops in Belgium, I was saddened when one of these beautiful Christians I met confessed to me that sometimes she didn't feel like she was a good enough Christian. On the day of my arrival to Belgium, I also heard something similar from a kind, young man who picked William and me up from the train station to drive us to Het Goede Boek, a Christian bookstore where William worked and lived in an apartment above. While driving, William informed me that this young man was a Christian, and the young man replied, "Yes, I'm a Christian, but not a very good one." I think I had felt the same way after watching the movie, _War Room_.[2] Later, in my workshop, Jenni, one of the participants, gave this insight when she quoted from Theodore Roosevelt: "Comparison is the thief of joy."

This reminds me of one day while I was babysitting my granddaughters, Penny, at age three and Vanessa at age eight months.

I had just finished eating lunch and was setting the dishes in the sink to soak. As I placed my empty bowl of chili my son had made into the sink, I remarked out loud, "Good job, Joshy," even though he was not at home.

Penny, across the room still eating her lunch, but having better hearing than I do, said, "Who's Joshy?"

I told her that's what I called her dad when he was younger.

She said, "Josh, is my dad."

I said, "Yes, he is." Then I informed her that he was my son, just like she is her mom and dad's daughter. I further explained, "When he was younger, I'd call him Josh, Joshua, or Joshy because he was and still is my son."

She heard the catchy sound in my voice from the love I have for him as my son and how wonderful I think he is. Then she said, "I want to have a son too."

I replied, "Maybe one day you will. You could also have a daughter."

But, with tears in her eyes, she cried, "I want to have a son now."

How do you explain to a three-year-old that this is not possible or really a very good idea even if it were? I tried my best when I said something like, "You need to wait to have a son until you're older and are married. You have a lot of growing to do before then." She still insisted that she wanted a son now, so, I continued, "Try to imagine yourself right now trying to take care of Vanessa all by yourself. She's too heavy for you to carry around. You'd have to be able to do everything for her, like change her diaper and make her a bottle. You're not ready to do that yet. One day, you will be able to, and you'll be a great mom. Right now, you just need to enjoy being a kid and keep on learning and growing."

I think God puts that desire in us to want to grow and become mature Christians. But I don't think he wants us to compare ourselves with those who are more mature and feel defeated that we aren't there yet. I think that can steal the joy we have in our current walk with Him. We need to trust in His plans for us.

Maybe we're just not ready yet, and He knows we have a lot of growing up to do before we can handle the greater responsibilities of being a mature Christian.

How can you feel joy with where you are at, but still strive to grow in faith and love for Him?

Have you ever considered the cost of being a Christian?

Just the other day, my mother-in-law brought me a beautiful, red rose, one of the lasts of the season. I remarked on its beauty and thanked her for sharing it with me. She informed me that it has a beautiful scent too. I lifted the bowl containing the rose to my nose and took a deep breath in. Nothing. I could smell nothing. I didn't want my mother-in-law feeling sad that I couldn't enjoy the rose to its fullest so I said something like, "It sure does."

WHO AM I?

The next morning, Rod asked, "Could you smell it?"

"No," I honestly answered.

He lifted the bowl to his nose and breathed in deeply. "Wow!" He exclaimed. "This really does have a wonderful scent! I can even smell it through my stuffed-up nose."

I've known for a long time that I really don't have much sense of smell. Sometimes it's a really blessed thing, as you can imagine. At other times, like this one, I sure wish I could smell better. My sense of smell is not as important to me as my sense of sight. If it were more important to me to be able to smell better, I'd really look into it and weigh the costs of what it would take.

In Luke 14: 25-35, Jesus gives a couple examples of why it's important to consider the cost of something before you decide to pursue it. In one example, he talks about building a tower, and how the builder, if he ran out of money after laying the foundation down was unable to complete the tower, would be ridiculed. He also talked about how, before engaging in battle, a king should decide whether or not he has enough funds to win a war. I believe Jesus is asking us to consider the cost of following Him. In Luke 9:23, Jesus tells his disciples, "Whoever wants to be my disciple must deny themselves and take up their cross daily and follow me." Are you willing to deny yourself and surrender everything to follow Jesus? How important is He to you? On a scale of 1 to 10, where would you put yourself as to how much you desire to surrender everything to follow Jesus? If it's not a 10, you can ask God, like I did, to help you get that kind of passion for Him in your life.

What is true wisdom?

Here is one of my prayers inspired by James 1:4-8:

WHO AM I?

Dear Daddy,

I want to persevere in my faith. I want the wisdom only You can give. I want to keep my eyes on You, Lord. Whenever fears or doubts come my way, help me to remember who You are and hold on tightly to Your promises. When I remain in You, the Devil will have no room. I will sing with the group, Hillsong United, "Not Today".

Prayer journaling has helped me to learn more about God, who He is, what He has done for us, and how He wants us to live. Whenever I have questions, He hears me and answers me. It may take time, but in some way, He reveals His truth to me. I believe He has answered my prayer and given me the beginning of wisdom. Proverbs 9:10 says, "The fear of the Lord is the beginning of wisdom, and knowledge of the Holy One is understanding." Through the working of the Holy Spirit and through meditating on His Word, I have come to fear

God because He has given me more knowledge and a better understanding of who He is and who I am.

Over and over again in the scriptures I see how God doesn't want us to have fear. Yet, it says in the Bible to fear God and keep His commands. So, I asked God what it means to fear Him, if it means to feel afraid. Then I googled the following question, "If Christians aren't supposed to fear anything then why should they fear God?"

When people have something they wonder about God, the first thing to do is go to Him in prayer. I will sometimes tell Him, "I think this means . . ., but what is the truth, what would You have me believe it means?" Then I ask Him to help me find understanding. Then I look at the verses in the Bible that mention what I am trying to find out. For example, when I was wondering what it means to fear God, I looked at all the Bible verses that mention fearing the Lord. Sometimes I grab a good devotional book on the topic of my question, ask my pastor, or maybe even find a few good Christian internet sites and compare what they say on the subject and cross-reference the information with Scripture to see if what they're saying is true. That's the process I go through when I have a theological or spiritual question.

Try this for yourself if you have the same question as I did or even a different question you may have. Has your thinking changed about what it means to fear God, or whatever else it was you were wondering about? If so, how?

Do you want to hear His voice?

"Here I am! I stand at the door and knock. If anyone hears my voice and opens the door, I will come in and eat with that person, and they with me." (Revelation 3:20)

I learned while preparing to give my first prayer journal workshop in Belgium that I hear God's voice in many ways: through His Word, through the convictions and prompting of the Holy Spirit, through messages from Christian leaders and authors, through conversations with His people, and through songs.

I now know that God's been speaking to me all along, and it hurts to realize that I was so busy focusing on the worries of this life that I didn't pay attention to Him. It reminds me of how it is for me sometimes when I'm writing and Rod starts talking to me. Instead of stopping and focusing on what he has to say, his voice is more like background noise, like the teacher in the cartoon show Charlie Brown. I really didn't hear what God was saying to me because I wasn't listening. I tuned Him out.

Please, God, I don't ever want to tune You out again. If I ever get so busy doing what I think I need to do, but You would rather have me be doing something else, please come tap me on the shoulder or somehow come between me and what I'm doing to get my full

attention. You are too important to me to tune You out.

If you do not think you are hearing God's voice, what wall do you think is keeping Him out? Will you ask Him to help tear it down?

Have you ever felt disappointed by the choices made by a Christian, or a group of Christians, you looked up to?

Sometimes people have the mistaken belief that mature Christians never have trials or temptations and are sin-free. They may put these Christians up on pedestals and when they fall off, they may question Christianity altogether. They may lose their hope of salvation.

We cannot base our faith on fellow Christians. We need to base it on the One and only, although fully human, He never sinned. Jesus Christ is our firm foundation and is the only One whom we should put our trust and faith in.[3] It is true that "Christ Himself gave the apostles, the prophets, the pastors, and teachers, to equip His people for works of service so that the body of Christ may be built up until we all reach unity in the faith and in the knowledge of the Son of God and become mature, attaining the whole measure of the fullness of Christ." (Ephesians 4:11-13)

We are to honor and respect our leaders.[4] But we also need to pray for our leaders. Satan would like nothing better than to get our leaders burned out on the pressure of trying to live to a higher standard than the rest of the church[5] and seeing so many people stuck in the muck of sin and trying to point them to Jesus. Satan will more than likely send many trials and temptations their way. They need our encouragement and support, just as much as we need theirs. Sometimes it's just a matter of reminding them to cast all their cares on the One who is in control of all things.

Yes, even mature Christians need reminders sometimes, but when they receive them, they are quick to open their hearts to the truth spoken with love and grace and go to the Lord in prayer and actually cast their cares away. There are some wonderful, on-line suggestions of how one can pray for their pastors. I believe we need each other. Our church leaders are a gift to us from Jesus to help us become mature Christians.

Going to a place of worship should not be something people do out of guilt because they think others expect it. We should be going to grow, to encourage and have fellowship with one another, and to share in communion with our Lord. Sure, I think churches, have hypocrites in them. I was one of them. Through a song, I was teaching the kids in Vacation Bible School the scripture verses from Proverbs 3:5-6 (NKJV): "Trust in the Lord with all your heart; Lean not on your own understanding; in all your ways acknowledge Him, and He will make your paths straight." At that time, was I truly trusting the

Lord with all my heart? Was I not leaning on my own understanding when I was not going to His Word or seeking Him to find the truth? Was I acknowledging Him when I thought I had to carry all my burdens myself and I was filled with depression and anxiety? Yep, I was a hypocrite.

That was a wall that kept my dad out of church for many years. He told me once, "They are nothing but a bunch of hypocrites." I was too young at the time to understand everything that had gone on between him and the church, but I remember hearing him say that, and then he stopped attending.

Many years later, after my dad retired, he and my mom began wintering in Florida where he began to attend church once more. He told me that the pastor was a true believer and lived by what he preached. After a few years, during the times he was back in Michigan, he began attending a Bible study group once a week. He got a study Bible for himself and bought one for each of us kids if we wanted one. I could tell how important reading the Scripture was to him. He admitted how stubborn he had been for so long and how much he needed to be spending time learning and fellowshipping with his brothers and sisters in Christ. When he became homebound because of his emphysema, he decided to make reaffirmation of faith and join the church his Bible study group was a part of. I, too, have learned the importance of coming together with my brothers and sisters in Christ. We tend to sharpen one another (see Proverbs 27:17).

I was hesitant about writing how important meeting with fellow believers, or what most refer to as "going to church", is. I thought perhaps people could infer the importance of meeting together from looking at how important hearing God speaking to me through my pastors, Dave Hansen, and Ben Stout, Jr., and talking with fellow believers has been for my growth as a Christian. I also thought that if my readers got into the scriptures more, they would see that God desires them to be involved with a community of believers.

God, however, affirmed that I should be writing about how important meeting with fellow believers is because at four o'clock one Sunday morning, He laid it on my heart to do so. Then later that same morning at church, Pastor Dave's sermon touched quite a bit on this subject. He added, "We are mutually broken; we are mutually needing of each other. We need to love one another because we are all in need of Him (Christ)." Look at Hebrews 10:24-25 where it says we need to come together to "spur one another on toward love and good deeds" and not give up meeting together, but to encourage one another. People can't do that in their own bedroom or wherever they are prayer journaling. Time alone with God is good, but He wants us to be in community with other Christians.

If you are not going to church, what wall do you think is keeping you away? Will you allow Jesus to knock it down?

If you are going to church, how have you experienced growth by listening to your pastor's preaching?

WHO AM I?

In what ways do you think you can show your pastor(s) you appreciate his/her (their) service?

How are you praying for your pastor(s)?

Are you following Jesus or are you dictating to Him where you want to go?

"My sheep listen to my voice; I know them, and they follow me." (John 10:27)

Dear Daddy,

This morning I was thinking about Penny and how smart she is, which I discovered through watching her learn. Just Thursday, I saw her holding the pencil too far near the eraser end. The line she drew was thin and not very controlled. I said, "Penny, if you want to have more control over where your pencil goes, you need to hold it closer to the tip." Then I showed her how. She had listened to me, watched what I showed her and did her best to follow my example.

One of the reasons why Penny listens to me is because she trusts me. She believed that I knew what I was talking about and could show her a better way. She trusted me that I wouldn't show her how to do something I didn't think she was capable of learning how to do. Another reason why Penny listened to me then was because she admitted to herself that she needed help, she desired to change her habit in order to obtain her goal, and she believed that she could, with my help. Lord, I believe this is what Jesus meant when He said, "Truly I tell you, unless you change and become like little children, you will never enter the

Kingdom of heaven." (Matthew 18:3)
She was being a good sheep.

Sometimes I think as Christians we are a lot like my yellow lab. He loves to go for walks with me, but I haven't trained him very well what it means to heel. He always thinks he needs to be leading the way a couple paces ahead of me. I think he's just so self-confident that he thinks he knows where we're going and is not dependent on me to show him the way. Eventually, I have to pull on the leash to get him to go where I need him to go. He needs to get better at following my lead. We need to get better at heeling too because although we think we know the way, Jesus doesn't always follow the path that we think is the way we're headed. He might want to turn in a different direction. When we get too far ahead, we don't realize He wants to go a different way. It's so much easier if we are walking beside Him or even a little behind Him to know where he wants to lead us. That's why He says, "Follow me."

This reminds me of a song by the group, 10th Avenue North, called "Control." All our good intentions can still fall short of the goal. We need to just follow where Jesus leads us. We are all unclean. All our righteous acts, apart from Christ, are like filthy rags.[6] People often do good things just for the world to see. No matter how good their deeds are, their intentions stem from their own selfish motives. We are to "look to the Lord and His strength; seek His face always (1 Chronicles 16:11)."

"Trust and Obey", the old hymn written by John H. Sammis along with Towner in 1887, keeps returning to my heart. This is what my testimony is all about. God has shown me the importance of trusting and obeying Jesus, listening to His voice, and doing what He's shown me or has asked me to do. As Jeremiah 17:7 says, "Blessed is the one who trusts in the LORD, whose confidence is in Him." Yes, I believe there is no other way to be happy in Jesus.

WHO AM I?

Have you been a wandering sheep or a pulling lab who keeps getting ahead of the Lord thinking you know the way? If so, are you ready to acknowledge Jesus as your Shepherd, your Master, your guiding Light? Let's pray.

Dear Jesus,

You are so patient and kind. You keep wooing us with Your love. You wait for us to come to You, to receive Your love and grace. You do not impose Yourself on us. You want us to receive You willingly. You don't give up on us. You do not want anyone of us to be lost. Help us to get rid of the wall of pride that stands in our way of us receiving Your grace. Help us to accept Your love, Your strength, and Your guidance in our lives. Help us learn to follow You.

In Your Name we pray, Amen.

Are you listening to the voice of truth or Satan's lies?

John 8:44 describes the devil as "a murderer from the beginning, not holding to the truth, for there is no truth in him. When he lies, he speaks his native language, for he is a liar and the father of lies."

Dear Daddy,

Is it wrong to feel ashamed of past sins when you know they are forgiven?

In an article called "When You Believe in God but Are Ashamed of Your Past" by Craig Groeschel,[7] I learned that Satan wants to use our past sins to make us feel defeated and live a life of unhealed pain, as if God doesn't exist. When we let shame control our actions, we can't live our lives for God. He gives

49

Peter denying Christ, his repentance
and God's forgiveness as an example of
a character-building, kingdom-victory
lesson.[8] "God wants to renew our hearts
and minds and to send us into His world
as lights shining in the darkness. Like
Peter, we can become convinced of the
truth: that we are not our sins. And
we're also not what others have done to
us."[9] Rather, Groeschel reminds us that
**"we are who God says we are: His
children."**[10]

Yes, God, that is what You
reminded me of in the prayer shack (a
small, gray shack in Honduras where I
once had prayed). I am forgivable,
changeable, capable, moldable and am
bound by Your limitless love.[11] I will
accept the things that cannot be
changed and not pretend I'm innocent
when I do wrong but be honest. I will not

allow Satan to bind me to the guilt trap and rob me – or You – of the joy I have found in a life redeemed and restored by You. I will put my hope in You and trust that You have made me a new creation, just as the verse You gave me in the prayer shack, 2 Corinthians 5:17, confirmed. Help me to reject what shame says to me and hear what You have to say. Because I know that You are working in all things – even my sins, past and present – to bring good in my life because I love You and have been called according to Your purpose.[12]

This reminds me of the song "Maybe It's OK" by We Are Messengers. What a freeing feeling it is to be able to come out of the shadows that my shame hid me in. Hallelujah! I am not dirty; I am clean!

I hope I have been transparent with my sins because I do not want to come across as "holier than thou," but as someone who is forgiven and so thankful for her renewed life.

God does give us a memory though. We don't forget where we came from, but we look forward to where we are going. One memory we should never forget is how deep, and wide and high the Father's love for us is and to hold on to the promises He gives us. This is what helps us turn away from sin and live a better and more holy life.

I can't go back and change the past, but that doesn't mean I can't encourage someone who's going through the same struggle. I used to think I couldn't say much because I had given in to temptation, and I would be a hypocrite for saying anything, especially now that it is no longer a temptation for me. I believe it is one of Satan's lies to keep us from helping each other. I've learned it's better for me to say, "Yep, I struggled with this temptation and sinned because I didn't put God first in my life. That's not what He wants for you and neither do I because I love you."

Like Pastor Ben says, "We need to be transparent. So, don't hide your shame or past mistakes, but show instead God's love and forgiveness and how to seek Him first."

Has there been a sin in your past that you have kept hidden out of shame? If so, how do you think God can use you to show others His love and forgiveness and how to seek Him first?

Yes, telling me I should hide my shame and still feel guilty for it, even though I knew God had forgiven me was one of Satan's lies that I believed. As Christians, when we hear the voice of doubt, we need to be prepared with the truth of who God is and be ready to defend our beliefs, or pray to God, as I have in the past, like the father of the dying child did in Mark 9:24, "I believe. Help my unbelief."

When writing this book, here are some of the lies I believe Satan tried on me: "Who do you think you are? You're nobody famous. To most people, you don't even have some big, life-changing event to write a story about. You are just an ordinary Christian. Why would anyone want to read about your life?" But I replied, "That's right!" And I started singing "Nobody" along with the group, Casting Crowns. It does not matter who I am, but whose I am. I am not writing for the world to see me, but to see God and how much He wants to restore humanity back into a right relationship with Him. Maybe by taking a look into how God has been at work in my life through prayer journaling, it will inspire others to have a closer walk with Him.

Sorry, Satan, you can't have that brick.

"Then, how about this one?" he asked. "You tried writing a book before. You sent it to all different publishers you thought might be interested in it. But it did not get printed. This will be just a waste of your time."

Really, Satan, that's all you've got?

It's partially true. That is what Satan's lies are. I did write a book a long time ago for a class I had taken when working toward my Early Childhood Endorsement. It was about a child (well, a mouse) who wanted to play the violin (which is one of the instruments I play), and how he was terrible at it while he was learning how to play. Nobody wanted to listen to him, but he kept on practicing anyhow, until eventually, everyone was surprised when they heard him play a solo for one of his school's performances. I did all of the illustrations myself.

I just had fun making that book for the class. But the professor said, "This is really good! You should try to get it published." I found out how to go about getting a story published, sent my drafts to various children's book publishers, but no one was interested in publishing it. I never wrote a book since until God placed it on my heart to write this one.

Sorry, Satan, but it will be worth it if it touches just one heart for Jesus, even if it never gets published. I know Jesus would leave the ninety-nine and go after the one.[13] Maybe the person reading (or writing) this book right now is that one.

Yes, I agree with We Are Messengers calling out, "The Devil is a Liar."

Thank you, Jesus, for setting me free and opening my eyes so I can see.

What lies has Satan ever told you? How can you defend your beliefs with the truth of God?

I hope you join me in adoring the Lord of heaven and earth and find it amazing that He cares about us and lights the path that we tend to wander from; that the One who sees all of our sins still looks on us with love; that the all-powerful, storm-calming, wall-demolishing God wants to take away all our fears and give us peace; that He hears us when we call to Him and calls us His child. Have you ever asked God, the same as the group Casting Crowns and I have, "Who Am I?"

GOD WON

3

Reckless Love

"The God who made the world and everything in it is the Lord of heaven and earth and does not live in temples built by human hands. And He is not served by human hands, as if He needed anything. Rather, He Himself gives everyone life and breath and everything else." (Acts 17:24-25)

Dear Daddy,

Penny asked me last weekend why God made people. "I don't know," I replied. "That's a good question." Others I know have asked the same question. In my search for an explanation, I was thinking about how sinful we are as people and that we don't love You the way You deserve to be worshiped and adored. I also considered that You knew from the beginning that we would be this way. The truth is, God, that You don't need me at all as I know from Acts 17:24-25 and the song "In Awe" by Hollyn. I learned so much from Dawson McAllister in His article, "Why Did God Create Us: He doesn't really need us, so why did he create anything?"[1] It was not because You were lonely. You already had company -Your Son and the Holy Spirit.[2] It was not because You needed Your ego fed — to satisfy some craving to be worshiped. You are totally secure in who You are — without us.

You chose to create us anyway out of Your great love. It says in Jeremiah 31:3 that You love us with an everlasting love. That means You loved us before we were even born.

You are love[3] and because of that love and Your wonderful creativity, You made us so we can enjoy all that You are and all that You have done.

Also, like Pastor Dave said, "God created us to fulfill His eternal plan. God in His infinite wisdom, chose to make us a part of His eternal plan."

What part do we play in that plan? There are all kinds of instructions in the Bible about how to live our lives. Pastor Dave shared in a sermon some Biblical instructions:

1) Loving God with all your heart and with all your soul and with all your strength.[4]

2) Loving your neighbor as yourself.[5]

3) Doing the good works which God prepared in advance for us to do.[6]

4) Fighting Satan's lies, for we're also part of the war between God and Satan and God's ultimate plan to defeat Satan. By putting our faith in God, we can defeat Satan and his lies.[7]

5) Pointing people to eternal life with God – through His Son, Jesus Christ. This is the most important part we play in God's eternal plan. We not only tell people of the wonderful opportunity they have to be made right with God through Jesus, but we live our lives in such a way that reflect our message. This is our ministry of reconciliation. It is urgent and vital, for it truly is a matter of life and death. We have a responsibility as Christ's ambassadors to implore people on Christ's behalf to be reconciled to God.[8]

GOD WON

Take note – we have a choice in all of this. When God created us, He did not make us pawns in some cosmic chess game or toy soldiers. God gives us freedom of choice.

Bottom line – God may not need us, but we clearly need Him.

Dear Daddy,

My prayer is that all people will choose to put their trust completely in You and play an exciting part in Your loving, eternal plan. 2 Peter 3:8-10 reminds us that You are patient, and You do not want anyone to perish, but everyone to come to repentance. Your love and patience are so overwhelming, God! I sing "Stand in Awe" with the group, Hillsong Worship, as I truly do stand in awe of You! Who can comprehend the depths of Your love?

RECKLESS LOVE

If Penny asks me again why God made people, I will simply say, "Because He loves us."

If you have been wondering, when and how I started prayer journaling, let me tell you my story.

In an old flour-grinding windmill in Holland, Michigan, as a young, Dutch-dancing girl and tour guide, I was asked by my boss, "Why are you always smiling?" I said, "I don't know." But later, as I reflected on it, I thought, "Silly Sheryl! You do know! It's Jesus that makes you so happy!"

Before I asked Jesus in my heart, I had once been a girl who wanted to be so liked by my two older sisters that I followed them around. Whenever they would let me hang out with them, I did whatever they were doing, even when I knew what they were doing was wrong. They are thirteen months apart. I am about two-and-a-half years younger than my middle sister.

God can use our experiences, good and bad, to lead us to Him. One memory that comes to mind happened one summer night when my parents had a cookout over a fire pit in our backyard for supper. Mom was cleaning up in the house afterward, and I think Dad had settled in on the couch. My sisters and some neighbor boys decided it would be a good idea to get the fire going again and roast some marshmallows over it. They sent me in to get the marshmallows while they worked on getting the fire built back up. After my mom left the kitchen, I sneaked into the cupboard and got the half bag of marshmallows. My sisters got the roasting sticks, and we all began toasting marshmallows. After the bag was emptied of marshmallows, one of the neighbor boys who was my older sisters' age, put the empty plastic bag on the roasting stick and held it over the fire. He flung the melted goop off, and it landed on our wooden picnic table. Young and naïve, I got scared that the picnic table was going to catch on fire. Consequently, I wiped it off with my left thumb. That burned so bad that I wiped my thumb on my right arm. Trance-like, I staggered into the house and matter-of-factly informed my mom that I had burned my arm. When she looked at my arm, she dropped what she was doing and rushed me to the hospital. I had a third-degree burn on my arm and a second-degree burn on my thumb. I still have the scar on my arm to this day. That scar serves as a reminder that I shouldn't allow myself to be led just to impress people. God wants me to seek Him, even if it isn't popular.

Sometimes people do not always have what's best for us in mind, unlike God. When I was nine years old, we were sitting on some cots, hanging out with my sisters' friends in a little, white shed my dad had built. As a cigarette was being passed around, one of my sisters encouraged me to take a puff. Because everyone was looking at me, I took the cigarette. I'm not sure if I even inhaled, and I didn't even care for the taste, but it was the beginning of a bad habit.

I do not want to mislead you into thinking that whenever I hung out with my sisters we always misbehaved. Quite often, we just hung out in the woods behind our house riding bikes. We made a figure-eight racetrack and would go around and around until we were all tired and ready to go home. We also built forts out of pine branches, and once we even dug an underground fort. I also have fond memories of our winter expeditions. We would head down our dead-end road, go across the railroad tracks, travel through the woods, as we carried our sleds to go down a tremendous hill. We'd zoom down and trek back up over and over again for hours. Mom always had hot chocolate and marshmallows ready for us when we got back home.

Sometimes my sisters just didn't want me around. They would go to their friends' house and not want me to come along. Sometimes they would have their friends over, and they wouldn't include me. I felt left out. I didn't realize, that with God, I am never alone. He wants to be included in every part of my life.

One summer, when I was 12 years old, my parents let me go to Cran-Hill Ranch, a Christian camp. I remember being led in discussions about Scripture with my camp counselor. Afterwards we were sent out to find our own little quiet spot in the woods. We were given a pre-made journal to answer questions and reflect on the Scriptures discussed in our group time. It was the first time I had done anything like that. Little did I know at the time what an important habit journaling would be to me many years later.

On our last night at camp, they did a consecration service. They talked about Jesus and how He died to save us from our sins. They asked if anyone wanted to accept Him into their heart. I felt this tugging on my heart and walked forward. Later, when I got home, I told my mom about it. She suggested that I go to the elders to talk to them so that I could make my confession of faith in front of the church. I remember sitting in the room with all these older gentlemen asking me all kinds of questions about my faith. It was with great joy, on the following Sunday, that I stood up when the minister called my name and asked me questions.

"Do you take Jesus as your Lord and Savior?"

I answered, "I do".

"Will you follow him with all of your heart?"

"I will."

One time after my confession of faith, I caught myself trying to sneak a pack of my dad's cigarettes. "*How could I have done such a thing?*" I thought. "*God wouldn't want me to steal.*" In anguish of my sin, I swore to myself that I would never smoke again. A while later, someone knowing that I had given up smoking, tried to get me to start up again by offering me one of her cigarettes. God gave me such joy for obeying Him when I turned down her offer. To this day, I feel blessed that I chose to obey.

At school, there were a lot of kids who smoked and drank. I chose not to hang out with them. I thought, "It's better to have no friends than bad friends." Instead, I found some kids in my church and at Youth for Christ to hang out with. A small group of us, from Youth for Christ, would go around from church to church some Sundays and sing. It was a great time!

When I was about fifteen, our leader at Youth for Christ was heading up a trip to Saint Vincent Island to help remodel a Christian school. It was a lot of money to go that had to be raised. I would have never thought it possible that I would be able to raise that kind of money. My church helped me out, we did a few fundraisers, and I know my parents assisted me quite a bit too. I will never forget my trip to Saint Vincent Island. We sang songs as we worked with the islanders. We tore down walls, built new ones, and then later painted them. We were there for three weeks. We took turns cleaning and cooking for each other. One Sunday, we ferried over to a church on a nearby island. The way they sang with their whole heart is burned into my memory.

A year or two later, I helped encourage our youth group to go on a mission trip to Kentucky to help fix up a Christian camp. Our mission leader was a great young man who was attending Hope College in Holland to become a youth pastor. He challenged us to apply the Scripture messages each evening into our lives as he led us in devotions and singing praises to the Lord. I have a few memories of the work of white washing walls and preparing meals for everyone, but the green hills of Kentucky always remind me of the quiet times I had there by a stream thinking of the Lord. This laid a foundation for my journaling. God was working on me, and I didn't even realize it. He is constantly laying the groundwork for our future growth even when we are unaware.

Before I became a Christian, I dreamed of saving the animals in Africa. I was going to be the one flying in a helicopter, shooting them with tranquilizers, tagging them and giving them medicine if they needed it. After I became a Christian, I had a fleeting thought, "I could go to Africa and help God save people rather than animals."

As years went by, I took a different path. In my junior year in high school, I decided to take a childcare course at the vocational center. I had enjoyed babysitting neighbor kids growing up. Hence, I thought this might make a great job for me to do. My teacher, after seeing the skills I had with planning lessons, encouraged me to become a teacher. I had never envisioned going to college. No one in my family had ever completed college before. The next year I did a work study program for a Title I Reading and Writing class for first through sixth grade students. I absolutely loved being a teacher's aide. Putting a fleeting dream of being a missionary in Africa away, I thought, "Well, if you want to become a teacher, you've got to go to college," so off I went.

College is where some of the walls that I didn't know I was building when I was younger started really taking shape. You see, when I was younger, I had been hurt by boys picking on me for my lack of physical development compared with other girls my age. When I grew up, I still found I didn't have a super-model-Barbie-doll figure. I had also been told I was clumsy by someone I loved, and I found myself still making silly mistakes. I felt like I didn't matter during the times when my sisters didn't want me hanging around. I frequently felt like the tag-along-who-nobody-wanted-around-in-case-she-tells-on-us, baby sister. I also had been praying for my dad to go to church with us, but it seemed as if God didn't hear my prayers. Feelings are deceptive. The Bible says, "The heart is deceitful above all things and beyond cure. Who can understand it?" (Jeremiah 17:9) These were the beginnings of my "I'm not good enough" and "I don't matter" walls.

In College, I became aware that young men were attracted to me. It flattered me, and it made me feel like maybe I was good enough physically. It led to immoral choices. Because of these choices, I ended up getting hurt and this not only strengthened my walls of "I'm not good enough," and "I don't matter," but it also caused me to begin building my "I need to have control" wall.

With God's grace, I got married to Rod. I had two wonderful sons, Josh and Corey, and after a few years of trying, I got a full-time teaching job (which in my mind was too long so it added to my "I'm not good enough" wall). My first year was really rough. I was trying to implement working in groups as I had been trained in college to do, but the kids were used to whole group instruction and then individually working on their assignments. I had not been trained how to implement new ideas slowly. The year added more layers to my "I'm not good enough" wall.

Through it all, I knew I needed a relationship with God. I knew going to His house of worship was important, so, we went.

After a time, we moved to Kent City, Michigan, where Josh and Corey spent most of their growing years. The church we attended in Casnovia did not have a Children's Worship ministry. When we brought the need for one to the attention of the minister, he encouraged a young couple to start one. We took turns weekly so they wouldn't have to lead it every Sunday. Then our family got involved with other ministries as well. We attended Sunday School before the church service. During the service Rod and I led the congregation in worship with the praise band. Sunday evenings would find our kids attending youth group. Every summer my teenage boys and I were involved with Daily Vacation Bible School. Throughout that week, I would lead the children in worship, and my boys would assist with learning stations. I even led a small youth group for a couple years. It was more of a Bible Study group, but we did a few extra outside fun things together too. One time we went to Chuckie Cheese and had a great time eating pizza and playing games. Another time we went to Michigan Adventures. We all enjoyed going on the big, swinging boat over and over again.

The reason I chose to write about all I had done for the ministry is not to brag. It's to show people that God, in His miraculous, gracious, merciful and loving way can use them no matter where they are in their walk with Him. I know this because one summer as a camp counselor at Cran-Hill Ranch, I had to teach the kids how to windsurf. Before camp started, we were given instructions on how to do it. I could get up and hang on and go, but I could never figure out how to get it to turn to go back. There were many times I had to get rescued on the other side of the small lake. Even though I couldn't properly windsurf, when I passed the exact instructions I had been given onto the kids, they could do it.

I am thinking that my walk with God for all those years was like my windsurfing. The walls I had built up were stopping me from freely being able to windsurf with God. I was stuck on the other side of the lake. I needed rescuing. Except, I did not even realize it. Yet, God has a kind of love that can kick down any wall we have built up by believing Satan's lies. Yes, He has a most wonderfully amazing, "Reckless Love" as Cory Asbury sings it.

GOD WON

4

Open the Eyes

of My Heart, Lord

"Many are the plans in a person's heart, but it is the Lord's purpose that prevails." (Proverbs 19:21)

Dear Daddy,

Today at Home Depot, I brought in my frame and picture of Psalm 46:10 and waited for one of the paint men to be free to talk. I wanted his opinion on whether staining or washing the frame with paint would get the desired effect I wanted before I made my purchase. He suggested the wash and added, "I like that verse."

I said, "Thanks! I do too. Many people stop or have memorized the first part, 'Be still and know that I am God.' They miss out on the most important part — 'I will be exalted among the nations. I will be exalted in the earth.' It's really all about God — not about us or what we need to do."

"Yes," he said, "We are here to glorify Him." Then he proceeded to tell me of how many people have blinders on their eyes — they are unwilling to admit there is a God.

Thank You, Daddy, for opening my eyes, to not only acknowledge that You exist, but that You are also in control. Thank You for reminding me that this is Your show. I sing along with

Twila Paris and praise you while singing "God is in Control."

One fall day, we had plans to go to a scholarship dinner with our son, Corey, who was attending Lake Superior State University in Sault St. Marie, Michigan. When he found out that his scholarship representative wasn't able to attend, he decided not to go. Since we had just spent the weekend before with him, we decided to go to Rod's family's auction of his grandma's and uncle's belongings instead. At the end of the auction, they announced they were going to put Rod's grandma's farm up for a silent auction, but it had to go for a fair price. We had a week to put in a sealed bid if we wanted to buy it.

Rod and I thought that one day when we retired, we would build a home on the forty acres we owned in White Cloud, Michigan. It had always been his dream to be a hobby farmer. That year, we had decided that we really liked living in Kent City, Michigan, and we had lots of good friends there. Because of that, we thought we'd remodel our home intending to make it our "forever" home. Our story shows how true Proverbs 1:9 is when it says, "In their hearts humans plan their course, but the LORD establishes their steps."

After the auction was finished, we drove to grandma's farm just to have a look at it. The original farm home had burned down years ago. In its place was a small modular home with a nice, metal roof, dilapidated porches, and an old, rusted door. Even though we could not get in to look around, we knew it was not worth much. There was also an old, much-less-to-be-desired garage with a tattered roof, broken doors and cracked windows. Before we walked the farm's forty acres, I looked around and just was not impressed by its scenery.

We have fond memories of our land in White Cloud and our two sons, Josh and Corey, going hunting and camping with us and the times that we had the Cub Scouts and family parties there. We also had so many memories in

Kent City with our boys growing up there and many friends close by. We could not afford to keep all three places, so we would have to give up our home in Kent City and our forty acres in the woods. The decision was not an easy one to make. If God really wanted us to move to the farm of Rod's grandmother, then I wanted to see the beauty this place had to offer. "If You would like us to live here, will you please make it beautiful for me?" I asked boldly.

The property had not been farmed in years and weeds had taken over. The house was hidden behind swamp land. There were some woods, but nothing like the forest on our other property. It had a few birch trees, beech, and white pine, all my favorites. Still I was not overwhelmed by its beauty. Then we walked up onto the only hill. I looked out across the road. Observing all the beautiful deciduous trees in all of their glorious fall colors, I nodded my head and admitted, "OK, God, You have made it beautiful for me."

As I reflect upon all my spiritual growth since I moved to Lakeview, Michigan, I really believe it was God's plan for us to move here, that He directed my steps to draw me closer to Him. After many years of driving thirty-seven miles to work, I was now only seven and a half miles away from the school where I was teaching. The funny thing is, I only stayed working there for another year and three-fourths. My plans were to retire when I turned fifty-five, but I was really struggling to maintain control of my classroom the year I turned fifty-three. It was a difficult class to begin with; however, by October, I felt really good about the way things were going. Sure, they kept me on my toes, but I thought we were headed in the right direction. Then a student moved in with her own emotional baggage and the behaviors that went with them. I just did not know how to work with her and maintain my classroom management or instruction. I was suffering from anxiety attacks.

Every morning before I headed to school, I'd be praying for help while I was working out. I did not feel effective as a teacher. I did not want to keep teaching just for the money and the good insurance. When I first started teaching, I vowed that if I ever got to that point, I would be done, no matter if I was at retirement age or not. I had talked to Rod, and we made financial arrangements in case I could not make it through the year. Besides this, Rod was overworked in the dental lab that he owns and needed some extra help. I was torn up inside. It was March. I hated the idea of leaving a class so near the end of the school year, but one morning before school began, my principal came to my room to talk. After a bit I sighed, "I just want to do what is best for the kids." She responded, "I don't know what is best for the kids." I knew then and there what I must do. I had suffered depression before. I foresaw that was where I was headed. So, after I got home from school, on a walk through the field, as tears streamed down my face, I prayed to God about it. Then, I wrote my two-weeks' notice for early retirement and sent it to the superintendent and the principal. That big storm in my life piled high the bricks on my "I'm not good enough" wall. Now, I was a quitter.

After I retired from teaching, I had much more free time, even though I was working full-time for Rod. Later that spring, I started to lead a small-group for church. Small-group is where we get together with a few other members of the church and discuss the previous Sunday's sermon. We try to see how we can apply it to our lives, and we share what we are thankful for and any struggles we have, and then close in prayer. It mainly included just Rod and I and another couple, Mike and Lori, but we also had other people come from time to time. We became very close friends with Mike and Lori.

One night, Lori shared with me her challenges with leading Children's Worship. I thought I might be of some help to her, but I really did not know if I wanted to work with kids again after what I had gone through. The "I'm not good enough" wall was blocking my way from offering to help her for quite a while, but I eventually did. One of the students who knew me from school said, "I know why you quit teaching. It's so you could teach here." I smiled and said, "Yes, I believe that's why." You see, the way I was while I was teaching that year, I would never have offered to work with kids in church.

Sometime later, Pastor Dave gave a sermon on prayer. It reminded me of the movie "*War Room*."[1] I felt a connection with the younger woman who had a hard time praying. The older woman who was deeply committed to praying showed the younger woman how she was being a lukewarm Christian. It hurt my heart to think of the possibility that I, too, was a lukewarm Christian because of how weak I perceived my prayer life to be. Jesus said in Revelation 3:16, "So, because you are lukewarm – neither hot nor cold – I am about to spit you out of my mouth." I did not want God to think of me like vomit in His mouth!

I knew I had to work on my relationship with God, so, during our next small-group time, Lori and I agreed that we should start prayer journaling. But did I just go right out the next day to buy one? Nope. Nor the day after that . . . or that . . . or that.

A few weeks later, Lori surprised me with my first prayer journal. "Thank you!" I exclaimed as I took the gift from her. However, inside I was thinking, *"Now I better start to use it."* For a whole year, I tried writing in it on a regular basis, but I wasn't consistent. There were weeks on end when not a word was written. I still prayed like I always had. Yet, God still used that prayer journal to draw me closer to Him.

I praise God that He is so loving and consistently faithful to us even though we are not. Thanks to God's leading, Pastor Ben asked me to help out at youth group. I was under the impression it was for one Sunday night, but I felt encouraged to keep on going. After a couple of gatherings, I felt inspired to grow in my relationship with God. One night after speaking about prayer, he sent me off with a small, mixed-aged group of teens to lead a discussion on prayer. I was grateful for the list of questions he gave me. One of the questions was, "When do you hear God speak to you?" One of the teens heartfully answered, "I hear God speak to me all the time."

That night I drove home a little sad because I didn't think I had ever heard God speak to me. I once heard a story about a woman who claimed to have heard God speak audibly to her. I thought, "It sure would be nice if He spoke audibly to me. Then, I would certainly do what He asked me to do."

Later, before climbing into bed I prayed, "I want to hear Your voice, God." In the morning before I woke up, the lyrics, "I hear your voice, God. I hear Your voice" in the song, "I Need You God" from the group, Consumed by Fire, was playing in my head. Filled with great joy, I felt it was God telling me that I do hear His voice and that He speaks, personally, to me through song because I am a musician. This thinking was challenged later. However, that morning I wrote:

Thank You for Your reassuring words in my sleep, Lord. I hear Your voice! You are a GREAT and AMAZING God!

Every morning after that, if there was a song in my head, I'd quickly jot it down in my journal. Then I would locate the lyrics online and reflect upon them in my journal, making them personal. God was using the Christian songs to draw me closer to Him. I was thinking of God and writing more frequently in my journal.

Another small-group night, Lori and I had discussed how we would like to go on a mission trip, but we didn't do anything about it. Later, Joyce, a friend of mine from my old church surprised me by asking me if I'd like to go on a mission trip with her to Honduras. A group of teachers were going to go there to share teaching strategies and the love of Jesus by leading a day of Vacation Bible School in a public school. How cool is that? Immediately, I said I'd like to go. Of course, I could not be fully committed to going until I had talked to Rod. He agreed because he loves me like Christ loves the church.

God still loved me too, even though I was a quitter. He loved me enough that I believe He sent me on that mission trip to Honduras.

The week before my mission trip to Honduras, I was volunteering as a counselor for our church's district Kids Camp. I had never worked with six- to eight-year-olds at an overnight camp before. Twice a day, we would have a large group time with singing, games, and a Bible message. After each session, we would break off with our cabin groups to discuss what they had learned. To be better equipped to lead these discussions, I began taking notes on my phone during the Bible messages. I had no idea God was showing me that I didn't always have to record my thoughts in a notebook, that a phone would do just as well. This came in very handy a little over a year later when I developed tendonitis in my thumb. More importantly, though, God was showing me how writing down what the pastor was saying would help me to remember better and how valuable that is for reflecting on the pastor's message and applying it to my life. More and more, I realized how necessary and valuable reflection is toward applying the message to my life.

A day after I got home from camp, I was headed to Honduras, with my journal packed in my bags. Watching God at work those ten days in Honduras amazed me. I recorded daily all that I had witnessed and experienced in my journal. On Monday, our first mission day in Honduras, Joyce and I decided to get up early and take a walk along the ocean. We saw these little holes on the beach. When we started walking along, these little ghost crabs scurried along and quickly dived into the holes. When they thought we weren't watching, they would crawl back out. On our way back, I noticed this small, old, wooden boat. Derogatively, I commented, "Joyce, I don't know about *you*, but *I* would never get in a boat like that in the ocean!" Joyce chuckled and agreed.

For our mission project that day, we were just part of the group helping put cement flooring in a student supply store at the school. We had to cross a picket line of transportation strikers in order to reach the school. They let us through when Dennis, one of our leaders who was from Honduras, explained what we were going to do.

After we helped out mixing and carrying cement for a while, a few of us planned to leave a bit early to go back for a meeting for abused women. One of our leaders, Carmen, a licensed psychologist, was going to give a talk about forgiveness to these women, and I was going to play my guitar while they worked on a craft. When we came to the only spot to cross to get back to where we needed to go, a different group of striking transportation men who were unaware of our morning's arrangements came running at our van. They began beating the van with cut-off limbs of trees because they thought our van was for tourists and we were breaking the strike. Anna, Dennis' wife, bravely rolled down her window and explained that we were missionaries and what we were doing there. They stopped beating the van, but they wouldn't let us through. We had to head back to the school, and we didn't know how we'd be able to go to the meeting. Anna contacted Dennis who was working on a different project. Because the school was on the ocean, he found a young man who would pick us up in his boat (yes, just like the one Joyce and I had seen earlier that morning) and take us around the road-block area (for a price).

Here is my journal entry for that night:

Dear Daddy,

The ghost crabs this morning reminded me of the fact that if we seek You through your Son, the Way, the Truth and the Life, we shall find You just as Joyce and I patiently sought after what had caused those holes in the beach. You are in all things and work through all things. You are an amazing God! About that boat business, you sure do have a sense of humor, God. You heard me say, "I don't know about you, Joyce, but I wouldn't want to be in a boat like that in the ocean," yet, later in the day because of the public transportation strike, there we were in a boat just like that! Thank You for taking my fears away when the men were attacking our van. I knew you would take care of us.

Our last mission project for our time in Honduras was at the public school we had worked at on Monday. We taught a day of Vacation Bible School (VBS). In the morning we taught Kindergarten through Fifth-grade students. After lunch, we taught the Sixth through Twelfth-grade students. We each had our own station with a translator. We were teaching the salvation story based on the colors in a salvation bracelet each student received: black for sin, red for Christ's blood, white for forgiveness, blue for baptism, green for growth, and gold for eternal life. We had three story-telling stations where they learned the meaning of one or two of the beads using flannel board illustrations or puppets. The message of the gold bead was taught through a craft as they made gold crowns because we will live and reign with Christ for eternity as sons and daughters of the Almighty.[8] We also had a snack station, a games station, and my music station, where I taught them Christian Kid songs sung in Spanish and in sign language. The kids were very excited, and some had tears in their eyes when they realized the sin in their lives. They also got to hear the good news of how our sins are forgiven in Christ when we accept Him as our Lord and Savior.

Here is my journal entry from that morning:

Dear Daddy,

I am so happy that the strike was called off for these two days so we will be able to do VBS at the school tomorrow. Please encourage my friends who may be feeling apprehensive about the VBS. Thank You for giving us the courage to do it in spite of any fears. I am not fearful, Daddy, because I know You will be with me. It will be as You have planned. Help me take advantage of any opportunity I have to share Your love.

Amen!

Here is my journal entry later that night:

Dear Daddy,

Thank You for being with us today at the school for VBS and keeping the evil one away. Thank You also that even though it was very hot, it didn't thunderstorm as it had been forecasted, and that the strike was put on hold. Therefore, we could still have the VBS without any problems. Bless all the volunteers from the local churches who helped in the kitchen and with the children. Thank You for their patience today. May this VBS inspire them to reach out more in their community.

Be with all of us tonight as we rest up from this exhausting day. Thank You for Your strength and courage today! I love You!

You see, I got to watch God do wonders, call off violent men, and postpone strikes, so we were able to accomplish all that we had come to do and more!

On the Saturday before we were flying home, however, I experienced a bad day. It was our day off, and I decided to go snorkeling with part of our group that morning. I grabbed some extra money to give as a tip. After we got back, I went to get my money out of my backpack. It was gone! I knew exactly which pocket I had put it in that morning, and I had no doubt it had been taken. Worst of all, when I brought it up to my friends, no one believed me. They thought I had just misplaced my money in my backpack. Now, you know a bit about me, because of my "I don't matter" wall, I did not speak up loudly or boldly about it. I just shrugged my shoulders and thought, "Well, they got their tip." A bit later at the pool, I went through my backpack again in front my friends. "Yep. No money," I declared, but still, no one believed me. I felt hurt. Later, I was sitting journaling in the bed that I shared with Joyce. She was on her iPad. Even though I didn't want to sound like a dripping faucet, I decided to say something to her again. Now, you have to give Joyce a break for not believing me. She's been around me long enough to know how frequently I lose things. Our two sons practically grew up together like brothers. Finally, she looked in her wallet and found that all of her money was gone. Then, she told the others and all of their money was gone too! Eventually and miraculously, we got back all of our money from one of the young men who took us out snorkeling.

In the afternoon, Rod sent me a picture of our granddaughter who was visiting grandpa with her dad at our home. I sure was missing all of them.

Just after supper, the leader asked us to prepare a Sunday School lesson for the next day. The leader suggested I do the same butterfly craft that I had done earlier that week with some kids at a church where we were laying cement and putting in electricity. I couldn't see how we would be able to have enough supplies to do it again. I also couldn't fathom how we could put together a well-thought-out lesson in just one night.

I just had to get out of there. I grabbed my water bottle and went for a walk. In my heart, I cried out to God that I just wanted to go home!

My walk brought me past a house on stilts that had some punching bags hanging underneath. "I just want to punch those bags!" I shouted at God. You see, not only was I feeling bad about my friends not believing me, but before our trip, we were asked to create a Sunday School lesson. Immediately, I thought of a craft that the kids in my Children's Worship group loved. It was a lighthouse out of a red solo cup, black duct tape for windows and a door, and a clear cup on the top with a battery-operated candle in it. I thought we could do a lesson on how Jesus is the light of the world. I shared my idea with the leaders, but not the whole group. Because I thought the other teachers were too busy teaching, I went ahead and planned out the whole lesson.

Meanwhile, a few weeks later, someone else came up with the idea that we should do a lesson on the fruit of the Spirit. Everyone agreed. I shared with the one who suggested the lesson my idea. Since everyone had agreed about her topic, however, I told her it's fine with me to just go ahead with the fruit of the Spirit lesson. The problem was that no one had prepared the lesson. Therefore, we didn't gather any materials for it. The leader decided we just wouldn't do a Sunday School lesson. Perhaps she had forgotten about my suggestion.

Maybe now you can see why I was frustrated. I was thinking, "If only she had said, 'Sheryl has a lesson; let's do hers.' I would have had enough supplies." I just wanted to go home, but I was stuck there.

I continued my walk because I wasn't ready to go back. Hence, when I saw a little, gray shack a short way off the road in a field, I decided to step inside. It had a cute, little bench to sit down on for a bit and just be with God and pray. My prayer went something like this: "God, you know my heart. You know how upset I am right now. I need You to create in me a clean heart."

After a little while, I heard God speaking to me through the book, Crazy Love by Francis

Chan.[2] The mission team had read and discussed this book prior to our trip. Chan gives an example of an extra in a movie who rented an entire theatre for family and friends to come and see a movie in which he would appear for only two-fifths of a second. He explains that people would think the extra was crazy if he thought the movie was all about him, but that's exactly what we tend to do sometimes.[3] God said to me, "Sheryl, you are a child of mine. You do matter. But *this ain't your show!*" It was like ice water being thrown in my face to wake me up. I knew God was speaking to me. Then He put the song "Move - Keep Walking" by Toby Mac on my heart. He was saying, "Get moving! You are not alone;[4] you are a part of the body of Christ.[5] Do your part. Be a worker![6]"

God used what seemed to me a bad day at the time and changed it into something good. He woke me up and opened my eyes to see the "I Need to Have Control" wall that had come between us. He grabbed ahold of a sledgehammer and gave a resounding "WHACK." This is His show, not mine.

I prayed, "Lord, please help me overcome my frustrations and give me ideas for tomorrow," and, of course, He did. He gave me a verse to go with the butterfly craft: 2 Corinthians 5:17, which says, "Therefore if anyone is in Christ, the new creation has come. The old has gone, the new is here!" When I found the Spanish version, he gave me the idea to make a poster of a butterfly and put each part of the verse on a wing. He gave me a tune to put the verse into a song and the idea to start out slow and sing it faster and faster. When I got back to the place we were staying, I was excited when we gathered together to make our plans for the Sunday School lesson. Everyone got a part to do and when we found we needed more sandwich bags for the craft and didn't have enough time to go to the store, people went to their suitcases and emptied out some bags they had brought along.

When I woke up the next morning, I wrote in my journal:

"I realize now how Satan had used my hurts from childhood of feeling left out and not wanted to get me to feel alone and insignificant. I thought that all I needed was God and no one else. I know that's not true. You want us to need other people as well, to teach us to get along and work together because You know that together we are whole.[7] I may be just a cell in the body of Christ, but I have a purpose and You can use me. Satan would love me to put up walls. Please, Lord, when I start doing that (again), help me to see Your truth and tear them down! We are not alone!"

Soon, we were on our way to church. After traveling quite a distance in an overcrowded, hot, humid van, we arrived at a pavilion-like church out in the mountains, far from the ocean. It was awesome seeing truck beds piled up with people coming to worship. The lesson was so much fun and well received. I felt so blessed by God that He had created in me a clean heart. I asked, and He'd given me what I needed and just enough bags too! That night I reflected:

"How blessed I was today for listening and obeying You yesterday!"

The next morning, I felt the Holy Spirit telling me that I should talk to Carmen about the disappointment I was having on Saturday. I still thought it was crazy to have to suddenly come up with a lesson the day before we had to present it while we had time before the trip to plan one. Normally, I wouldn't do this. I'd just forgive what appeared to me to be a lack of organization without confronting and go on with life. However, when I asked her about it, she told me that they really hadn't planned on doing a Sunday School lesson before we came. She went on to say that just that Saturday, while Dennis was traveling through town, a pastor who had worked with him the week before we arrived, flagged him down. He pleaded that their church needed to have Carmen share a message on unity in marriage because many families were struggling with this. That is why we promptly had to come up with a lesson. God had opened my eyes. Moreover, He made it clear to me that a lesson on butterflies is more appropriate for children that live in the mountains than a lesson on a lighthouse would be. I finally could acknowledge that God is sovereign.

It wasn't until after I acknowledged that God is in control and His plans are higher than mine that my prayer journaling took on a whole different aspect. It appears to me that this lack of acknowledgment was another thing that was stopping me from freely windsurfing with God. After that, God opened my eyes up to Scripture, and I began meditating on His written Word in my prayer journal.

Thank you so much, Daddy, for hearing and answering my plea to "Open the Eyes of My Heart" just as Michael W. Smith sings. I can see You!

5

God is on the Move

"Create in me a pure heart, O God, and renew a steadfast spirit within me. Do not cast me from Your presence or take Your Holy Spirit from me. Restore to me the joy of Your salvation and grant me a willing spirit, to sustain me." (Psalm 51:10-12)

Dear Daddy,

Thank you for the joy of Your salvation and having Your Spirit living in me! It is 1:00 a.m. and You are speaking to me, Lord. Here I am! I am praying for ------. Whatever roadblock she has that is stopping her from giving herself completely to you – fear- remove it! Let her trust in You for her salvation. Let her not fear death but know that neither life nor death can separate her from Your love. Help her to love You more than life here on this earth. You are life, Lord! I remember one time in church singing "Bring the Rain" by the group, Mercy Me, and thinking, "Oh, I know God is with me in/during/through the storms, but why ask Him to bring one on? I don't think I want to do that." Not much later, I read an article about a nineteen-year-old man who got swept out to sea for 10 hours. After his rescue, he got to tell the world how he talked to You the whole time that he was out in the sea. He joked it was not a great vacation, but the most exciting one he's ever had – one he'll never forget. Then it hit me – Your light shines brightest in the darkness. It is like not being able to see if a flashlight is turned on in a lit room, but that same flashlight sure brings light in the darkness! I want Your glory to be made known in this dark world we live in. If that means You allow me to go through rough waters so I can share Your glory with others, so be it. Thank You for the storms You brought us through in Honduras, Lord!

Storm 1 - When the strikers blocked the road and began beating on the van, I was not afraid. I knew You were with us no matter what happened. And You were. You brought us a boat. You also lifted the storm on Friday so that we could do the Vacation Bible School. LET YOUR LIGHT SHINE BRIGHT!

Storm 2 – When I faced the roadblock of my self-pity, I told myself that nobody believed me and that nobody cared what I thought or cared about my ideas. Satan was opening a can of worms (lies) and wanting me to eat them.

You came and You spoke to me with Your still, small voice through Your Word hidden in my heart and the songs You placed there.

I do matter! But this ain't <u>my</u> show- it's Yours! I am here to bring You praise and share Your glory with others. You are glorious, Lord!

I asked You to renew my attitude, and You did! You gave me 2 Corinthians 5:17! You gave me "Move (Keep Walking)" by Toby Mac. You gave me all those ideas of ways to teach the kids how to hide the Word of God in their hearts. Your Word of life set me free. I am free to worship You with all my heart and free to bask in Your presence. Thank You, Jesus, for sending Your Holy Spirit to me to reveal these truths to me! Thank You, God, for Your Word of life!

I do not care whether I live or die. (*Readers, don't get me wrong. I do want to live, but I want to live for Christ. I meant that I am not afraid of dying because I know that it will be even better for me. I will be seeing my Savior face to face.*) Either way, I will sing Your praises! Whatever Your will is for my life, Lord, let it be done! All I ask is that it bring You glory and praise, so everyone knows it's all about you – no denying!

Some people might just say – well, you were just there doing self-talk. I know differently! There is no way I'd ever say it's OK with me to go through tough times; I'd like to avoid them at all cost. Your Spirit gave me that desire and courage to say, "Bring on the heavy rains, if that's your will, if it brings You glory, praise, or points people to You." How about this: could I have "willed" for our money to be returned or for the strike to cease? NO. All good things come from you alone (James 1:17).

My old self would have called someone who would agree with me and help me justify my attitude when I didn't want to help with the Sunday school lesson. Then I would have stayed hard hearted. Instead, I followed Your Holy Spirit calling me to pour my heart out to You and seek what You had to say. You gave me a whole new attitude and great desire to work on the lesson.

Then there are the ideas You planted in my heart when I was in Honduras. I had this strong desire for when I got back home to talk to the

Children's Worship team. I considered
it necessary to find ways to hide Your
Word deeper in the children's hearts
so they might not sin against You. The
week I got back, my friend texted me
and asked if I could meet on Sunday for
a Children's Worship team meeting.

Self-talk – I DON'T THINK SO!

Wow! God! Thank You for being
so obvious!

I pleaded, "I want to hear Your
voice. I want to grow closer to You." I
wanted to know it was really You
speaking to me, not just self-talk. You
answered me that night I first prayed
that through a song, "I Need You God"
by Consumed by Fire. I knew then that
You do speak to me and often through
song. I kept listening for Your voice. I did
not want to miss what You had to say to
me.

Yes, here I am at 3:00 a.m., writing this all down because You placed this on my heart. I know Rod probably thinks I'm crazy. (He came in to check on me. Bless his heart!) I guess I am crazy – crazy for You!

I'm overwhelmed by You! I am <u>in awe</u> of You! Dear Jesus, what You did for me and for all of those who believe – every day I fail, I am a compulsive sinner, but You have covered my sins with Your blood – Your love is truly overwhelming!

GOD WON

I can stand confidently in front of
You, God, on judgment day because You
are in me and Your Holy Spirit will make
me pure – white as snow! You have
made a way for me, Jesus! Oh yeah!
Blessed be Your Name, God, for You
loved us so much that You sent Your Son
to not only die for us but to live in us! I
am filled with Your Spirit. I do not want
my life filled with sin, just as I wouldn't
want my garden taken up with
knotweed. I wouldn't want any of that
in my garden because once it's in there,
it'll take over, and it's pretty difficult to
get rid of. I know that right now the Holy
Spirit is like a herd of grazing goats (a
solution that can help get rid of
knotweed). The Holy Spirit is helping me
to deal with the sin in my life and give
me strength in the face of temptation,
and one day, Satan's schemes will all be
completely eradicated! What a blessed

day! I can't wait! But, Lord, I will wait on You! Even in the shadows, I know You are there. If You want me to go to heaven to be with You, I'll go gladly. If You want me to stay, even if all I can do is breathe and praise You, so be it! Your will be done! Overcome any desires that lead me astray from what You would have me do. Let me be Your witness, Lord!

Let Your counsel, O Jehovah, stand in my heart – Let it be my treasure. (Prayer based on Psalm 33:11)

Proverbs 4:25 reflection - My eyes tend to wander. Lord, keep them focused on You and on things eternal! Help me be a strong, brave warrior for You. If I fix my eyes on You, Jesus, I will not be overwhelmed by my circumstances, problems, challenges, or feelings. I will not fear opposition. Let faith rise up! Let me grab a hold of that shield and make me unshakeable!

When I am right with You, God, I feel so alive and unshakeable!

Help me to keep Your commandments – to love others as You love them and above all else, to love You with my whole heart. Fill me with Your wisdom and understanding. Keep my feet on your straight path and help me to run without stumbling. Help me to hold on to your instruction and not let it go. It is what brings me life. Let Your light in me shine bright. Help me to listen to what You have to say. Help me to guard my heart against Satan's arrows. Help me to guard my tongue. Help me to persevere and stay the course. Amen!

One of the first questions Lyssa asked me when I got to Belgium was, "When were you saved?" "I don't know," was my reply. "I think it was when I was twelve years old." I was struggling with the knowledge that God had somehow moved in my heart relatively recently to increase my desire to seek to do His will versus my own will. Lyssa asked if I had had a life-changing moment when I was twelve. I told her I had, explaining what I was like before and then after.

In order to answer that first question properly, I think we must first look at the definition of "being saved." From Elizabeth Haworth's article, "The Three Elements of Salvation,"[1] I concluded that God's unique gift of salvation given to us by grace, exhibits three distinct facets that can only be seen through faith.

One facet is the point and time when we are born again by believing in Jesus and declaring that He is our Lord (Romans 10:9). We are "saved" because we no longer have to pay the penalty for our sin, which is eternal separation from God. Instead of having to pay our debt for our sin, we receive God's mercy and are clothed with Jesus' righteousness. Because of this justification, we can no longer be accused. Pastor Dave explains it as follows: "God sees us just as if we had never sinned." Justification is the bridge to a relationship with God.

The second facet of salvation shows us a lifelong process, namely our "sanctification." That process has ensured that as Christians we are freed from the power of sin unto this day, and we are continually molded into Christ's image. Although it is God's will to sanctify all of His children, we must still choose daily to present ourselves as a living sacrifice, holy, and pleasing to God (Romans 12:1). Dr. Alan Redpath explains what being holy, or consecrated to God, is: "It is living in harmony with the passion in the heart of God for a world that is lost . . . . It is not a question simply of trying to empty your heart and life of every worldly desire – what an awful impossibility! It is rather opening your heart wide to all the love of God in Christ, and letting that love just sweep through you . . . till your heart is filled with love."[2] As we submit more and more to the guidance of the Holy Spirit following Jesus' example, "we are blessed with continued deliverance from the power of sin," said Haworth.[3]

The final facet of salvation brings us to the resurrection of our body. When that takes place, we will be like Him, for we will see Him as He is.[4]

God wants to save us all, but why? In John 3:16 it is written that God does not want us to perish, but rather to have eternal life. Does that mean that God wants to forgive our sins so that we can all go to heaven instead of hell? Possibly, but perhaps He is referring to more than we can imagine. Andrew Wommack boldly states in his article, "Eternal Life There's More to It Than You Think," that, **"If all you did was ask Jesus to forgive your sins so you wouldn't perish in hell, then you are missing**

out on eternal life."[5] John 17:3 teaches us what eternal life really means, namely: knowing the only true God, and Him whom He sent: Jesus Christ. Wommack tries to explain exactly what "to know" means in the Bible. In Genesis 4:1 (the King James version), we read that Adam "knew" his wife, Eve, and that consequently Eve conceived and gave birth to a son. Adam must have known Eve intimately. God, our wonderful Creator, wants us to know Him intimately, and that is why He sent Jesus to save us.

When we have a trusting and loving relationship with God, we look at things more from His perspective. Instead of desiring to sin, we will hate it. We will admit when we have made a deliberate choice to do what we know is wrong and will want to resist doing it again, because we know how God looks at it and how much He wants us to live godly lives and overcome sin. This is confirmed in Revelation 2:7: "To the one who is victorious, I (Jesus) will give the right to eat from the tree of life, which is in the paradise of God."

Some people when reading 1 Corinthians 3:15 may think this means that they don't have to change how they are living. They can just continue in their sin without listening and obeying God because they think God will forgive them, and they will go to heaven regardless. When they sin, they may get the attitude of, "Oh well, that's just the way I am. I'm only human." Yet, when you look at the verse in context by reading from verse one in 1 Corinthians 3 to verse 15, you can see it's talking about the jobs people do for the ministry of building Christ's Church. In verse 10, we see that what we do for the Lord, we are only able to do by the grace of God. I believe He sets the task before us and gives us whatever we need to accomplish it, but many verses in Scripture refer to the effort we put into the tasks we are given. Even if that task is to be at peace with everyone and to be holy as in Hebrews 12:14, we are to "make every effort." Out of our love for God, we will strive to do as He desires and pursue to know Him and to grow in His life.

In Luke 3: 15-17, we read how John the Baptist told the people who were wondering if he was the Messiah, that he was not. He said that he baptized them with water, but that Jesus would baptize with the Holy Spirit and fire. Then John told of how Jesus has his winnowing fork in His hand to clear His threshing floor and to gather the wheat into His barn, but He will burn up the chaff with unquenchable fire. The Holy Spirit's job of transforming sanctification is to lead and empower us to learn obedience to the Word of God, and to conform us into the image of Christ.[6] Our good works don't save us. It's only through the working of the Holy Spirit in our lives and our belief in Jesus Christ that can save us.

This reminds me of watching Travis DeWall, a blacksmith and good friend of Pastor Ben. He showed those who attended Kids Camp during the summer of 2019 how he makes iron take the shape he wants. In order to do this, he sticks the iron bar in a very hot fire until it is glowing red. Then he puts it on an anvil and hits it with a hammer until the glowing starts to fade. After that, he sticks the bar back in the flames. He does this over and over and over again until it finally takes the shape of whatever he wants it to be. For the group that I was leading, he made a little leaf.

I feel like my will to do what I want to do, instead of doing what God wants me to do, is as strong as an iron bar. God has to heat me up, like He does when I burn with the shame of my sin. This gives me the desire to confess my sin, to seek His forgiveness and grace, as well as the forgiveness of those I have sinned against, and to continue to do my utmost to change my sinful habits and thoughts and to seek to do *His* will and not my own. I believe that every time I overcome a temptation to sin, there is a big rejoicing in heaven and in me. It's like taking a bite out of the Tree of Life. One day, I'll be able to eat the whole fruit! Hallelujah! Thank You, Jesus, for Your saving power in my life!

126

As I look back deep into my past, I can see how God heated me up to refine me. Let me tell you a story of his transforming power. One day, when my oldest son, Josh, was about eight or nine months old, I went shopping. As I stood in front of a stack of blue kiddie pools, I thought, "I should get one of these for Josh." Then I heard this voice say, "I bet if you took two, the salesclerk would never know." I did not even need or want two pools. I don't even know why this thought popped into my head, except to say that since I believe in God-prompts now, that this was a Satan-prompt.

When I was a kid, there was someone I knew who had stolen something once and her parents never found out. I was appalled at the time for knowing she did this, and I was disgusted by the fact that she had gotten away with it. That is why I do not understand why I listened to Satan's suggestion. I took two pools to see if he was right, and he was. The salesclerk just charged me for one. I took my ill-gotten good home, which was a little less than a half-hour away. By the time Rod came home, I was burning with shame because the Holy Spirit had been convicting me of my sin. To save face, I told Rod that I had "accidentally" taken two pools instead of one and that I was going to bring one back. He said we could keep it for the dog. I insisted on going back to the store and paying for the pool, regardless.

God was reminding me that even though other people might not know of my sin, He does. Satan never tempted me in that way ever again.

Years later, when our boys were in Cub Scouts, we had the leaders and their kids over to our house one night. The kids were playing games in the living room while the grownups sat around our kitchen table playing a game of "Scruples." In this game, you take turns reading a card that has a sticky situation and a given response to the situation. All players secretly decide how they would answer the question by putting a card face down on the table. The card reader has to guess how each person answered the question ("Yes," "No," or "Depends").

Then the players show how they answered. The card reader can challenge the players' answers, but the rest of the group gets an opportunity to help defend the person's choice or give evidence against them. Then everyone votes to determine whether they think the person was answering truthfully or not.

My husband's co-Cub Scout leader, and great friend, Tim, was the card reader. The situation was that a salesclerk had given you too much money back. The question we needed to answer was, would you let the salesclerk know. I picked the "Yes" card. Tim challenged me. Rod defended me by telling the story of how I had "accidentally" gotten two pools one time at the store and drove all the way back from Dorr to Wyoming, Michigan, to return the money for it. Everyone voted, and I won the challenge. Inside, I burned with shame over the fact that my husband was defending my honesty with the lie I had told him. Later that night, after everyone was gone, and Rod and I were lying in bed, I confessed my sin to Rod. His immediate forgiveness blessed my troubled soul. Later, I also told my boys about what I had done, but I never told Tim.

Tim was impressed by my honesty that night. Yes, I did answer the question honestly because I had been transformed by the Holy Spirit not to take what was not rightfully mine again. He saw the conviction in my answer even though my husband's defense was not truly a good example of my honesty. Since then I have seen the work of the Holy Spirit in Tim's life. He started questioning things, reading his Bible daily, and drawing nearer to the Lord. I found this out at his funeral. Tim was killed by a drunk driver at the age of forty-two. We miss Tim. Even so, praise be to the Lord! We will be rejoicing with Tim in heaven one day in the presence of our Lord and Savior!

As I now look back on my time in Honduras, I can see God's transforming power once again. After my mission trip, I knew something had changed in me. I felt such joy.

God urged me to develop a picture I had taken of the prayer shack and put Psalm 46:10 on it: "Be still and know that I am God; I will be exalted among the nations; I will be exalted in the earth." I found an old barn-wood frame, washed it to match the color of the shack, and hung my memorial up in my living room. This makes me think now of how God told Joshua to build a memorial of the time that the Jordan River stopped flowing when the Ark of the Lord's Covenant went across. He told them to build it out of twelve stones, one for each of the tribes of Israel. It was to answer their children's questions of what those stones mean.

One day, when the song, "Changed" by Jordan Feliz came on the radio, my heart made such a strong connection. I just wanted to dance as I sang along. A few days later, I felt a great desire to make a collage by getting pictures of a caterpillar turning into a morpho butterfly. I saw one of these butterflies in Honduras amongst the flowers by the shack. I typed 2 Corinthians 5:17 on it: "Therefore if anyone is in Christ, the new creation has come; The old has gone, the new is here!"

Shortly after that, however, I became confused because I knew that I had accepted the Lord into my life when I was twelve years old. Didn't I become a new creature then? What had changed in me? Hadn't I always loved the Lord?

On my fifty-fifth birthday, a little over five months after my experience in the shack, I realized how God was trying to answer my questions about my transformation. It was quite an eye-opener. Let me tell you about it. Rod and I had just returned from Fuji Yama, a wonderful Japanese steakhouse in Grand Rapids, after celebrating my birthday with a nice dinner. As we sat down on the couch, Rod grabbed the remote control as usual, and I began my knitting. Ordinarily, I don't care what is on the television. That night, however, when Rod started flipping through the channels, I thought it would be nice to view a movie for a change instead of the customary crime shows. Since it was my birthday, I thought it was my right to choose what we watched. Hence, I paid close attention while he continued switching the stations. When he came to one presenting a movie, I piped up, "That looks like a good show to watch." He said, "I suppose you would like to see that show," and continued to cruise the stations until he ended up watching "The Big Bang Theory." I just sat there fuming inside while he was laughing at their silly jokes.

After a while, I stood up and walked away arrogantly thinking a very unpleasant name for my husband. A name I don't care to repeat, and one that I have never used before or since. I don't even remember where I was headed, but I remember coming to a dead stop in our entranceway when I heard the Holy Spirit's voice say, "That's you, Sheryl before you submitted to Me. You are like the *((%$#@ sitting on the couch with the remote control in your hand when you don't submit to Me. You want Me to sit beside you watching whatever you want to watch. You don't want to ask Me what I might want to watch in case it is something you don't want to watch. You want Me sitting beside you and being there for you whenever you think you need Me, like the time when I helped you forgive someone who had hurt another member of your family and you couldn't do it on your own. There was also the time when you called out for Me in desperation when you were suffering with depression and hearing Satan's voice saying that you would be better off dead. Yes, when you cried out in Jesus' Name for him to be gone, I sent him away and you never heard from him again. You were able to enjoy the rest of your boys' growing up years and now you are enjoying your grandchild (and grandchildren to be). I did that for you. I care about you. You matter to me, but as I said in Honduras, and I'm going to keep on reminding you as needed, 'This ain't your show!' That is what I showed you in the prayer shack. That is what your memorial is all about. I am God, and you are not.[7] You need to give up the remote!"

God moved in me to show me how my heart had been deceived. I thought I was following God. I thought that I loved Him. I thought that I had made Him Lord of my life. Sometimes, I even thought the problem with people was that they knew who Jesus is, and that He died to save us from our sins, but they didn't make Him LORD of their lives. They just lived their lives the way they wanted to, instead of being obedient to Him. I was a hypocrite and didn't even realize it. I was the one who needed to make Him LORD of my life.

I was thinking that I chose to try my best to love God and to get to know Him better, which truly is the case, but I was holding back a part of me from completely trusting Him. I trusted Jesus that He would save me from my sins and let me go to heaven. Yet, I didn't completely trust God that He was looking out for my good here on earth. It would be like being married to a man who you didn't believe could handle money very well. You think he spends it on things he shouldn't. When you try to discuss it with him, he doesn't change because he doesn't think the same way as you. You either learn to live with him the way he is, you leave him, or you try to somehow take control of the finances. Regardless of the choice you make, your lack of trust does not make you unified in your marriage and you will not have the same peace as two people living in one accord.

In that prayer shack in Honduras, God made me realize my lack of trust and my sin of trying to take control of my life. He knew I wouldn't want Him to think that He doesn't matter to me, and He used that to change me. I would begin asking Him about what He wanted me to do and start listening for His voice. As I have come to trust Him more, even though I have a greater awareness of my sin, I have an even greater sense of peace. He has also given me His desire to share His love with others.

I really debated whether to share the story of the remote because I don't want anyone thinking less of Rod than the kind, loving husband that he is. I've never thought of him as that name before or since. I'm not sure, but I think somehow that event may have taken place to give me this shocking revelation. Rod is so supportive of me, that he even allowed me to put this story in here.

Lyssa had suggested that maybe I had just had a big growth spurt around the time of my Honduras mission trip. I think she is right, but I also believe Jesus saved me again, and He keeps on saving me. He is my Rescuer[8] and my Savior.[9] He is the Light of the World.[10] We are called to walk in His Light.[11] Thanks to the Holy Spirit, I experienced this big growth spurt. That's why I could draw closer to the Light. By meditating on God's Word and submitting to the work of the Holy Spirit, we can experience the nearness of God.[12]

It reminds me of working in the dental lab for Rod. In order to protect a severely damaged tooth against further decay, the dentist can place a crown on that tooth. The dentist first preps the tooth that will be crowned. Then he takes an impression including the prepped tooth and the surrounding teeth and sends it to a dental lab. There the crown is created. After the model of the impression is completed, it is my job to cut around the model of the tooth that has been prepped for a crown. The result, thereof, is called a die. This portion then becomes removable from the rest of the model.

I grind the excess stone off the die to get to the margin of the prepped tooth. Grinding creates a lot of dust and debris on the die. I use an air hose to blow off all the dust. Still, some clings to it. It's important to remove any debris because otherwise, the die might stick up too high when placed back with the rest of the model. When this happens, the completed crown will be too short. Therefore, it will not be in contact with its opposing tooth. With no contact, it won't be able to do the job of grinding or tearing the food effectively. Sometimes I have to take a brush to the die or a little pick in order to get out all the loose particles.

I used to work at a different workstation where the light was not as brilliant. Then Rod pointed out a bit brighter place. That new place made a big difference in my work. A huge smile appeared on my face when Rod shared this with me because I was thinking, "That's just how God works, when we draw closer to the Light, we see better how far we fall short of His glory.

Some people want to run and hide because they don't want their sins exposed. I want to draw as close as I can so He can help me see what walls need to be torn down. In order to do this, we need to humble ourselves and submit to God. We need to resist the devil. We need to come near to God, and He promises He will come near to us. We need to wash our hands and purify our hearts and stop being double-minded. Instead, we need to be fully devoted to Him. It can be a painful process, but He promises that He will lift us up.[13]

I believe Jesus worked in my heart to give me the desire to draw near to Him, the Light, and to be willing to brush, pick, or do whatever it takes to get rid of all my debris because He doesn't want any walls to come between God and me. Jesus wants me to fulfill God's divine purpose for my life. That's why He will keep chipping away at those bricks until none remain.

I could see how God was chipping away at my bricks during a time when He led me to read Ezekiel 36 which showed the Israelites pleading with God to be merciful to them. I got stuck on the word "profane" and just had to find out what the deeper meaning of it was. I wondered, "How had the Israelites profaned God's Name? Have I profaned God's Name?"

God was moving in my heart to bring to awareness that I had profaned His Name. This was heart wrenching because as a Christian, you know that, in God's view, this is a serious matter.

All these years I have been very careful trying to not use God's Name improperly. I would never say "Jesus" as an explicative or even "Oh, God," and it really bothered me when others did. I think I was deceiving myself, however, when I thought I did not profane the Name of God. I have really come to believe there is a deeper meaning to profanity. Anytime we treat God in a way that doesn't acknowledge His greatness, fear Him, and honor Him, then we are profaning His Name.[14] An example of this is when we choose to disobey God when we know that what we are doing displeases Him. Every time I speak or do something, it should reflect who God is because I say that I am a Christian. Because I am a child of God, I should give my utmost for His Name's sake to act like one.

I also agree with Joel Stucki in his article called "Two Common Misuses of God's Name"[15] which suggests if someone claims that God has spoken to them, but they really are only speaking their own words, then they are taking God's Name in vain.[16] When I told Pastor

Rachel that I thought God wanted me to write this book, I almost started to cry because I feared that my heart had deceived me and that God had not actually called me to do this. Which is why I had Pastor Dave and William look it over first for Biblical soundness. It's very important to me that my words speak the truth about God because I do not want to give people false teachings.

God doesn't leave us stranded in our guilt and shame when we find out where we have sinned. He gives us hope for the future and promises us that we can change, and that He will help us when we come to Him. Through my prayer journaling and through writing this book, I can see how He helped me change. These were the exact heart-felt pleas I had written in my first journal (the one I didn't think I was very good at keeping):

God, I pray that I can give up myself for your will to be done in my life.

God, I need you to tear down my
walls.

When I came across these prayers while
going back through my journals, which was
something I hadn't done until writing this book,
I bowed down in amazement of God. He had
been answering those prayers all along through
our time spent together. I felt affirmed in my
calling to write this book about how He tore
down those walls through prayer journaling.
Whether a Christian prayer journals or not,
looking back and seeing how God has worked in
your life strengthens your faith. You can believe
God's promises you can find in His Word. We
can trust that He who started a good work in us
will finish it and not give up on us.[17]

God has drawn me closer and closer to
Him. Seeking Him, knowing Who He is, and
trusting Him and His goodness, has made it so
much easier for me to give up myself for His will
to be done in my life. When there is complete
surrender, God can tear down the walls we have

built in our lives. We can then turn away from Satan's lies and listen, rather, to His voice.

He is a God who keeps His promises. Just as He fulfilled Israel's plea in Ezekiel 36, He satisfied mine. He does it for His Holy Name. He does not want His Name to be profaned. If we put our trust in Him, He will save us from all uncleanness. He allows us to cry out to Him, so He can take away our hearts of stone and give us hearts of flesh. We will be made new!

If you have already accepted Jesus as your Lord and Savior, and you want to live a godly life that reflects Christ, please pray with me:

Oh, God, please help me not to profane Your Name! Please give me the help and strength I need to fight my old sinful nature so I can live my life according to Your will. I want to be an obedient child that glorifies Your Name! I cry out to You, Abba, Father!

In Jesus' Name I pray, Amen!

Through my prayer journaling, God has shown me areas that need to be cleaned up in my life to make me debris-free, to help me not profane His Name. One area that needed lots of brushing away was my attitude toward Rod. I came to realize that I had not been treating Rod with the honor and respect that he deserves.

One occasion happened when I was bringing a friend to the Chicago O'Hare International airport. I thought it would be a good idea when I was in Chicago, Illinois to give water and snacks to the homeless near the Hyatt Regency where we go every year for dental conventions. I've walked those roads many times alone. I had no fear, but I knew Rod wouldn't like me doing this, so, I didn't tell him of my intentions. I thought I was doing something that would please God. I thought I was putting God first before my desire to please my husband.

God kept me safe as I stepped along with a loaded backpack down Division Avenue heading toward Michigan Avenue. I had a great time delivering the water and snacks to the homeless. After my backpack was empty, I strode with a purposeful stride unafraid and light-hearted as I found my way back to the car.

On my drive home, I called Rod and confessed what I had done. Let's just say, he was not too happy with my choice. Later when we talked about it before we went to sleep, I realized that I had broken Rod's trust. How was he supposed to know when I headed somewhere again that I wouldn't do something crazy or unsafe? What if something had happened to me? He couldn't even pray ahead of time or consider if I should do such a thing.

After reading devotionals about what unity in marriage is all about, I realized that if I prioritized unity in marriage, then I would please

God. The more I discovered what my role of being Rod's wife means, the more I recognized that what I had done had truly displeased God. My heart had deceived me. Marriage is supposed to reflect the unity between Christ and the church. Just as Christ is the head of the church, Rod is the head in our marriage.[18] Since he is a Christian, I know he won't ask me to do something or not do something that goes against God. Hence, if Rod doesn't think I should do something, then I better not do it. If he weren't a Christian, and I truly believed he was asking me to go against God's will, I would have to tell him respectfully that God's will in my life is priority.

I have also learned from my studies about unity in marriage of how important it is not to be a nagging wife.[19] Rod says I really haven't nagged much in the past. I know, however, that when I feel that the Holy Spirit has put something in my heart to do, and I really need Rod's agreement, it's awfully tempting to want to return to the subject if he doesn't give me an answer right away. I've learned that the best thing to do is pray about it and let the Holy Spirit convict Rod's heart if it needs to change or mine so we can be on the same page.

Through my prayer journaling, God chipped away at the bricks in my "Need to Control" wall. He did this by revealing to me that I need to cast *all* my fears on Him instead of wrestling with Him.[20]

We all have certain worries, or fears, that seem to sneak up on us. Perhaps that's the reason why the Bible says "Fear not," "Be anxious for nothing," etc. so many times. Our worries stem from our desire to control our environment or to control the outcome of a situation. In some instances, worrying can be beneficial. It can cause us to take action. For instance, a teacher is worried about the education the children receive. That is why he tries to plan and prepare his lessons so they would go smoothly. He thinks about what might go wrong during the lesson and put things in place to avoid those pitfalls. Worrying can also help us prepare for negative experiences in our lives. An example may be of how we may worry that our house may catch on fire and our children could be in danger, so we buy good smoke detectors and teach our children what to do when they hear a smoke alarm go off. Sometimes worrying can even give us a greater appreciation for the positive experiences in our lives. Someone may be worried the night before a surgery of how it will turn out. After a successful operation, he is even more appreciative.

Nevertheless, God still wants us to come to Him to lay our worries down. If we find we're having a difficult time leaving our worries at the foot of the cross, we have to consider why we're so anxious. Many times it happens when we want to change things that are not ours to change, or when we know that what we do or say does not please God.

Even though we know that anxiety is never healthy for us emotionally, mentally, or physically, we may find ourselves often anxious. It's a dark place where you spend more hours than you'd like to in a place that is filled with worrisome thoughts that are difficult to control.

Like the group, Casting Crown sings about in the song "Oh My Soul," when we find ourselves in that dark place of fear, we must face our fears and give them to the God we know. That's the time we realize that we didn't trust God enough while He is worthy of all our trust. We didn't lean on His goodness and love. We did not trust in His sovereignty, His mercy, compassion, grace and forgiveness. Oh, ouch! That hurts! The truth does sometimes because we love God and want to trust Him so badly. We cannot imagine what our life would be like without Him. We do not want the wall of mistrust to come between us and God. Rather than turning away from Him in shame and continuing in our worrisome ways, we need to turn and face the One who loves us. We need to confess to Him our anxious thoughts. We need to ask Him for His help to remove all doubt and fear. We need to cry out like the father of the boy with an evil spirit we read about in Mark 9:24: "I believe; help my unbelief!"

I must confess, I've had my share of fears. Let me tell you about one of them. Because I had grandmothers on both sides of the family get Alzheimer's disease (AD), I had this great fear of getting AD someday in my old age too. It seemed I was not alone. According to an analysis of a national survey taken in 2013 in the United States, next to the fear of getting cancer (40.3% of respondents), fear of getting AD/dementia was the next biggest condition feared (17.5% of respondents). The survey also found that women were significantly more worried about getting AD/dementia than men.[21]

It was this fear that drove me to journaling years ago on a trip out west. This was a different kind of journaling. I would write down stories of events that had happened in my life and my reflections on them. I thought it was a great way to pass the time on this long drive. I was hoping that, should I get dementia, having this journal read to me would remind me of who I was.

Then, after reading a book about a woman with Alzheimer's, I came to think how painful it would be for Rod and my family to care for me while I couldn't remember who they were. Worrying over this had me contemplating ways of how I could "accidentally" end my life if I should be diagnosed with AD/dementia. This way I wouldn't come to the point where I couldn't remember anyone anymore.

God has shown me how foolish that thinking was, and it's not because people with early AD/dementia are incapable of making that decision. There are cases where people in early dementia have opted for suicide.[22] It's foolish because my body is God's temple. Who am I to destroy it? I am not my own, for I was bought with a price.[23] Jesus paid that price for me, and He came to give me life, and life to the full.[24]

Yes, God has shown me how foolish taking my own life would be, but not only that, He has taken away my fear of getting Alzheimer's. He has told me that no matter what, I will still be His child and will be alright. He will get my family and me through the suffering (1 Corinthians 10:13). Even then He could use me one way or another for His glory. He has given me peace and hope for the future.

So, when was I saved? I accepted the Lord into my life at the age of twelve, and I am convinced that He who began a good work in me is still working for my good. Hallelujah! My spirit worships with the group, 7eventh Time Down, singing, "God is on the move!"

GOD WON

6

Lord, I Need You

"Simon Peter answered Him, "Lord, to whom shall we go? You have the words of eternal life. We have come to believe and to know that You are the Holy One of God." (John 6:68-69)

God, I know I can't do this life on my own. I need You so! Thank You for letting me hear Your voice. I don't want to lose sight of You. Your grace never fails me. Help me to humble myself. Your voice, Your grace, Your heart, Your love – I need everything of You! Just like the group Consumed by Fire, "I Need You, God." Together with them, I'm going to lift my hands up and breathe You in because I need You in everything I think, say or do, God! Let Your Spirit rule and reign in me. Your ways are higher than mine!

Becoming mature in faith resembles the feeling I had when I was a young woman graduating from college, getting a job, and getting married. Yes! I made it! I'm truly an adult now! I've grown up! It's so exciting, yet also terrifying, because once you are there and you realize your true dependence on God, you don't ever want to go back to the way you were. It reminds me of the movie called "Awakenings"[1] that is based on a true story. (Spoiler Alert) John Vogel, a movie reviewer, summarizes the movie as follows: "A new doctor finds himself with a ward full of catatonic patients. He is disturbed by them and the fact that they have been catatonic for decades with no hope of any cure. When he finds a possible chemical cure, he gets permission to try it on one of them. When the first patient awakes, he is now well into his fifties having gone into a catatonic state at twenty years of age. The film then delights in the new awareness of the patients and then on the reactions of their relatives to the changes in the newly awakened."[2] . . . Only the cure does not last.

Unlike the cure, God's Spirit does last in my life, and I know that I truly need Him for my salvation. However, there is still a battle between God and Satan for my soul as long I live here on earth.

Jesus warns us frequently to be on guard. Sometimes I really struggle with people's opinions or information I read on the internet when I'm looking for answers about questions that I may have in regard to Christianity. One time I came across a blog that criticized some Christian music groups because of the beliefs they held on faith, healing, and on their thinking that God wants us to be rich. Many of the songs that we sing in church and I listen to on Christian radio channels are written by some of these music groups. I wondered if I should even be listening to certain Christian radio stations. If they are playing songs written by artists that may not have biblical views than it's better not to listen to them. I told Rod about it over dinner one night. Astonished, he said, "But you LOVE listening to Christian music."

"I know," I replied as tears piled up in my eyes. "But I also know how songs can affect how we believe, and I don't want to listen to anything that goes against my beliefs. I don't think God would want me to."

I stopped listening to Christian music for a while. I even emailed my pastor about it. I investigated different radio stations to see what their beliefs were. I was happy to find that my local radio station, Family Life Radio, shares my same basic, fundamental beliefs about Christianity. Yet, I was skeptical because of the fact that they were playing songs written by those songwriters who were criticized in that blog, so I emailed the Music Director. Through her reply, discussing it with my pastor, and my prayerful consideration, I concluded that it is okay to listen to these songs because the songwriters share in our common fundamental beliefs which are reflected in their lyrics. But, by no means, should we make idols of Christian songwriters. They are humans. We must listen with discernment. I believe I had to go through this confusing time so God could steer me on the right path. He taught me to see that He doesn't only use songs when He speaks to me. The Bible surely talks about the importance of worshiping God through song. Moreover, Christian songs have played a vital role in my life as a Christian. They have been an expression of gratitude and the longings of my heart and a way of moving me to have a sense of awe and wonder in the presence of God. They help focus my thoughts on Him, rather than on me. They have also contributed to my spiritual growth. When I'm writing in my prayer journal and reflecting upon God's Word, often an old Christian hymn, a children's worship song, or some contemporary Christian song will come into my mind. I just start worshiping God by looking it up on my phone and reading the lyrics and singing along. I have seen that through music, people can understand the character of God and the Christian life more easily.

As a Christian, we need to not only be on guard for how Satan can use people's views, but also how he can use scripture references, like he did with Jesus.[3] Satan tries to get us to fear and keep our walls up. Luke 14:34 says, "Salt is good, but if it loses its saltiness, how can it be made salty again?" Satan kept telling me that Jesus couldn't change me. I could never be made good enough to be with God. He tried to persuade me that it was too late. I had willfully disobeyed God when I made those immoral choices in college, and that is what made me lose my saltiness.

I knew deep in my heart that I must not believe this lie because I remembered hearing God speak to me in the prayer shack in Hondurus. He called me His child. Since I am a parent myself, I know that I would never turn my back on my child if he apologized to me for something he did wrong. I would gladly accept his apology and not hold his sins against him. Of course, there may be consequences that he'd have to endure for a time, but our relationship would be unhindered. If me, being human can do that, how much more so can my heavenly Father forgive me and welcome me into His loving arms? Listen to what Jesus says in Luke 15:11-32 when He tells the story about the prodigal son. The father threw a party when his son returned home. Also, look at how patient God was with the Israelites and kept waiting for them to turn to Him even after they had willfully disobeyed. In 1 John 1:9, God promises us that "If we confess our sins, He is faithful and just and will forgive us our sins and purify us from all unrighteousness." Jesus also says in Mark 11:24 that "whatever you ask for in prayer, believe that you have received it, and it will be yours." I asked to have a burning passion for Him, and I believe I have received it. So, how can salt be made salty again? On my own, I could not do it. However, I believe God can do anything. As Jeremiah 32:17 says, "Ah, Sovereign LORD, you have made the heavens and the earth by Your great power and outstretched arm. Nothing is too hard for You."

Sorry, Satan, the mortar you've been using has cracks and has been exposed to Living Water thus it no longer has any strength.

Yes, there is a battle between God and Satan over our souls. I do not want to be God's enemy. I want to fight the good fight and choose to put on God's armor daily. This reminds me of Jamie Kimmett's song, "Prize Worth Fighting For." I prepare for the good fight by following what Jesus asked me to do in Matthew 11:29 when He said, "Take my yoke upon you and learn from me, for I am gentle and humble in heart, and you will find rest for your souls." When oxen are yoked together it makes them work as a team. It makes the task easier. Jesus wants us to be one with Him: one team. When we are heading in the same direction with the same goal in mind, our burdens are lightened, and we are able to find rest for our souls. He wants us to learn from Him. I believe He wants to teach us how to be gentle and humble in heart, just as He is. I have found so much peace and rest for my soul when I listen and obey what He tells me to do.

Let me tell you a story about how awesome it is to be yoked with Jesus, to be working as a team with Him. Back in January, 2019, Pastor Dave gave a sermon of trampling the waves with Jesus. He challenged us to get out of the boat. Earlier that week, I had been browsing the library for a DVD, and I passed over one with something about Africa on it. Around the same time, I felt God had laid it on my heart to share my testimony abroad. Some missionaries heading to Africa had visited our church once. "Maybe they could use my help," I thought. But I didn't know the language, and I didn't want to be an extra burden for the missionaries. When I talked to Pastor Dave about it, he asked, "Have you considered going to Belgium?"

"Belgium?" I thought. "No, why Belgium?" I asked. He reminded me about some other missionaries who run a Christian bookstore in Belgium that had come to our church asking regular Christians to come over and help. I did not even remember their visit, but Rod did. I went home and considered it. I thought, "Well, I'm a regular Christian." Then, I sent William and Lyssa an email about myself to see if they would like my help. They wrote back that they would. I asked Rod what time of the year would be less busy for work. He said September. William and Lyssa also said September was a good time for them. They were even startled, when they heard I had booked my flight before they had a chance to consider what

I would be doing to help them. Months went by without any communication. William and Lyssa were very busy with the running of their store and visiting surrounding churches for ministry and book sales. Instead of ordering their books on-line, Christians from local churches bought books from William and Lyssa's book table because that way they would help keep the bookstore open. The bookstore being open is a ministry in itself. People walk by and read the displayed verse of the day. Those who come in are treated to a free cup of coffee or tea and get blessed with a kind, listening ear and encouragement through prayer. Some Christians just come to hang out with other Christians since there are so few in Belgium. A few people stop in to find out more about what Christians believe. They hear the gospel message.

Just before I was scheduled to arrive in Belgium, William and Lyssa had a new ministry opportunity. This required them to move to Brussels, and it also meant learning, yet again, another language, French. They had already needed to learn Dutch six years ago when they first came to Belgium. This all meant that William and Lyssa would be packing up and moving during my visit because they already had plans to come to America a week after I was to leave. Therefore, I would probably be helping them pack up and move.

Before I came to Belgium, I told Lyssa that I like to do prayer journaling. She suggested that I do a couple of workshops at the bookstore. I was very excited about the opportunity to encourage other Christians to draw nearer to the Lord perhaps in this way. However, three weeks before my trip, my knee began giving me trouble. I had been preparing to ride a bike for when I got to Belgium. Now, I could hardly go up and down stairs, besides ride a bike.

One day, while doing pick up and deliveries for the lab, I found myself at the office of one of our long-time friends. I gave in to the temptation to complain about my knee and shared my worries about being able to ride in a car on a seventeen-hour trip to Maine. Rod and I had been planning that trip for several months with our friends, Rick and Joyce (Yes, the same Joyce that traveled with me to Honduras). I added my Belgium bike-riding concerns to my list of complaints, which was scheduled two weeks after our return from Maine. One of the first questions Lyssa had asked me before I booked my ticket was if I could ride a bike. In Belgium many people ride a bike when traveling short distances. "No problem," I answered. Now, just a few weeks before I was to go, it was a big problem.

What was I to do? I went back to the lab, and since Rod didn't need me at that time, I started studying for the Children's Worship lesson I was going to teach that Sunday. It was on the parting of the Red Sea. The Israelites had been complaining because they thought they were at a dead end. Literally, that's what they thought. They were doomed. They were trapped between a sea and a strong, Egyptian army with chariots and horses, but Moses told them not to be afraid, but wait patiently. The Lord would fight for them. They needed only to be still.[4] "Wow, God," I thought. "This lesson is not only for the kids, but for me as well. You want me to stop being anxious about my knee. I will cast my cares on You and stop grumbling. I know that you are in control. You can send anyone to Belgium to be a light there. It doesn't have to be me. If it is Your desire for me to go, You will make it possible. Otherwise, I will be content not to go." (Yes, even if it meant forfeiting the price I paid for my flight.) Peace, instant peace, came over me. Later, I met up with my friend to tell her I was sorry to have been complaining to her and that I should not have been complaining when what I really should have been doing was praying to God and trusting Him with my cares. I used to be worried about things a lot and didn't cast my cares on God and leave them there, trusting Him to take care of me. I had little faith. I still have trouble with that sometimes. The lesson of the Israelites' complaining when coming to the Red Sea was God's gentle reminder to cast my cares on Him and trust Him. He's got this. Because of the greater faith He gave me, I was able to cast my cares on Him. Because of the greater faith He gave me, it was made possible to do. That is why I had such peace. The way God gently corrects us is awesome.

I went online to find out what may have caused my knee pain. I concluded that I had patella femoral syndrome. Since I had physical therapy before, I knew exercise would be the best solution. Because I wanted to save money and time, I looked up on-line what exercises to do for this ailment. Every day I did those exercises, but when it came time for my annual physical, my knee pain had made no improvements. I informed my physician about my trips to Maine and Belgium. After she had looked at my knee, she advised me to go to an orthopedic doctor to get a shot in my knee. I asked for a referral to see a physical therapist instead. Because of my previous successful treatments, I knew that physical therapy was what I needed for healing. A shot would just cover up the pain. It would not heal my knee.

Before our trip to Maine, I had a few wonderful treatments at a local facility. My therapist agreed with my self-diagnosis. As I showed her the exercises I had been doing at home, she showed me how I was doing them incorrectly and demonstrated the proper techniques. She also taught me other exercises I could do on my vacation.

I had faithfully done my therapist's suggested exercises morning and night and was able to walk all over the place in Bar Harbor, Maine. My knee didn't kill me on the long ride home as it had during my ride to Maine. When I returned home, I was able to go to therapy a couple more times before my trip to Belgium. I knew during my trip in Maine that my knee was going to be okay for Belgium, and this was the case. When I got back from my blessed trip to Belgium, I went one more time to therapy for my final evaluation and dismissal. The therapist said, "I give all the credit to you for doing all the exercises as prescribed." However, the credit does not belong to me. Without God, I could not have done it. I tried doing it on my own, but God knew I needed expert advice. I thanked them for their time and for showing me what to do. It is a lot like how God works in our lives. The Holy Spirit gives us the training we need. Without His guidance and empowerment we would flounder in our calling to follow Christ and live a righteous life.

Because William's new ministry required him to travel for over three hours a day, Lyssa was left to run the bookstore by herself with a few volunteers. They had no time to pack their belongings. I was glad to be there to help. I also believe God used my prayer journaling workshop to encourage the people who came, including myself. I was able to share about how God had changed my life through spending time in prayer and in the Word. I also imparted some of the ways God speaks to me, mainly by means of: His word, the prompting of the Holy Spirit, messages from Christian leaders and authors, conversations with other Christians, and through songs. People asked questions and also shared about their personal faith experiences and revelations from the Lord. A few participants told about what brought them to the workshop, and I was able to pray with some about their personal concerns.

Then, God did this crazy thing. On Saturday, after a successful move and a few days before I had to leave, Jerry, a friend of William's, asked us to spend the night at his home. We were going to do a book sale at a nearby church the next day. The wonderful thing was, his wife, Awa, was from Gambia, Africa! That night, she cooked us an authentic African dinner! I got to talk to her as she prepared the meal. We also listened to African music during the preparations.

During dinner, William asked how Awa's family was doing. She showed us pictures of them. In one picture we could see that a roof had collapsed in one of their homes. A storm had damaged it a long time ago. However, due to a shortage of funds, it had been left in disrepair. God spoke to me that this was an African family that I could help.

The next day at church, I also got to meet and talk with Marvin, a Nigerian painter who is doing mission work in Belgium. During his sessions, he teaches people different painting techniques and shares the gospel with them.

God is so good! He answered my prayer about not being a burden to the missionaries and being able to encourage fellow Christians in their walk with the Lord. Besides that, He threw in my desire to meet and assist people from Africa! How awesome is that!!! Yet, the more I consider his love, the more I realize that our adoption as children of God is our biggest blessing.[5] He assures us that we will be resurrected and made in the image of Christ and share in His inheritance. Those are prizes worth fighting for. May we gladly take up the yoke of Christ for He assures us victory over our battles. Tell me, why would I ever want to go back to carrying the heavyweight of sin, doubt, and guilt again?

Because that's what walls are. When we believe Satan's lies, and when we seek our own desires instead of God's desires, it separates us from God. That is what sin does.[6] If I walk with Jesus and learn from His example of spending time alone with the Father and live life through prayer, I will be prepared for the daily fight and keep those walls from being built back up again.

Am I done yet? As I was writing this book, I kept thinking I was done, but even after I turned it over to my wonderful proofreaders, Pastor Dave, his wife, Sara, William, and my sister-in-law, Delia, I felt God urging me to write more. It made me think of the revision mantra I taught my first-grade students: "When you think you are done, you have only just begun." Even though the Word of God never changes, every time I read it, I always know there's something else I could learn.

One night at youth group the students were watching a theme, or word study, created by The Bible Project. The Bible Project also makes other YouTube videos that summarize each unique book of the Bible and demonstrate how these books fit into God's overall storyline of the whole Bible. We viewed the study on sin, which is "Khata" in Hebrew.[7] According to Collins and Mackie, the presenters of the Bible Project, "Sin is failure to love and honor God and people in the way that they deserve."[8] I agree. Sin is breaking the first and greatest command that Jesus taught us in Matthew 22:37-39 to "Love the Lord your God with all your heart and with all your soul and with all your mind." And the second: "Love your neighbor as yourself."

When you are a Christian, it can be discouraging when you fail to love God and others as you should, especially if it is the same old sin that causes this to happen. Satan likes to use this discouragement to push us behind our "I'm not good enough" wall from God. This reminds me of a song by Tauren Wells called "God's Not Done with You." I sure wish I was done sinning, but, as Sara, my pastor's wife, reminded me one day, God knows I can't handle being confronted with the load of my sins all at once. Therefore, He shows them to me, little by little, to teach me how to rid myself of them. I am looking forward to the day when my faith will be made complete, and my heart, mind, and will is in 100 percent alignment to His will.[9] Until that day, I'll press on toward the goal to win the prize.[10]

Here is an example of one of my recent sins:

One early-fall day, I knew that I had to pick and wash the tomatoes, and it was God's will for me to do that. The Spirit reminded me of this chore right when I was in the middle of writing. When I'm focused on a project, I hate interruptions, so I gave Him the big BUT. "But, God, I'm working on this book right now. Isn't this what You asked me to do?" God said, "There is a time for everything." I could work on it later, but my strong-willed, sinful self continued to write regardless. I think this happens to many Christians, but that's no excuse. Psalm 66:18 says, "If I had cherished sin in my heart, the Lord would not have listened."

We cannot go on sinning and saying, "Ah, that's just the way I am." We need to ask God to give us the wisdom, strength, and determination we need to be on guard for that sin and not want to keep it around in our life. We all need to think: "When I come to God, is it proudly with my own interests in mind, or do I come to Him humbly thinking about my sin the way he thinks of it?"[11] God sees sin as something very evil and hurtful. It displeases Him and others when we sin. Therefore, whatever the costs, we should fight against sin. When we look from God's perspective, then sin will become more evident, and we will ask for forgiveness more often. However, receiving forgiveness does not mean we are exempt from the consequences of sin.[12]

What were the consequences of me not picking and washing the tomatoes when the Spirit asked me to? Later that day, when I decided I had time to pick the tomatoes, it was dark out already. Then I realized that there is a specific time for everything and also for my book. The next day we had to pick the tomatoes, and my husband was not happy with that because he had put in long hours of work all week. In my devotions the next day, God gave me Proverbs 15:31, which says, "Whoever heeds life-giving correction will be at home among the wise."

God says in Genesis 4:7: "If you do what is right, will you not be accepted? But if you do not do what is right, sin is crouching at your door; it desires to have you, but you must rule over it." When Christians lose their balance and fall off the windsurfer, we are supposed to repent and accept the consequences of our actions. Moreover, Christians ask God for wisdom, strength and determination so that they can be on guard for that same sin. Then they get back on the windsurfer and keep moving on. I think that's what Scripture refers to as perseverance.

The words to the old hymn, "I Know Whom I Have Believed" by Daniel W. Whittle speak true for my heart. I believe "He is able to keep that which I've committed unto Him against that day." I believe that God has given me as a gift, so to speak, to Jesus.[13] Since Jesus loves God so much, wouldn't He take care of the gift given to Him? I also believe that the Father wouldn't give His Son worthless junk. I also know that Satan comes to steal and kill and destroy.[14] He would like nothing better than to break the bond we have with the Father. He is the greatest deceiver.[15] Hallelujah! Praise God! Jesus has come so that we may have life to the full, and now He pleads for us to the Father.[16]

I believe God works among us so that we can act according to His will and according to His good purposes.[17] I know people have been praying for me, and I know God answers prayer. I believe because of the prayers of His people, He made my heart sensitive to I hear His voice. Now it's up to me to be open to it and obey it.

God works in us, not because we deserve it. God's love and forgiveness is not for sale. His holiness and perfection cannot be equaled. If God had not sent His Son Jesus to bear the punishment for our sins, then we would forever be hopelessly separated from God. Thanks to Jesus' sacrifice we can go to the Father in prayer. If I was left to fend for myself, I would just go on sinning and building up walls. Yet, His Spirit living in me will never let us go. He keeps urging me to come closer, closer, closer still.

Even when we sin, God confirms that He loves us by pointing out the sin to us and convincing us of the fact that we are forgiven and renewed in Jesus. With His help, we can overcome our sins. I believe in the power of prayer. That is why I continue to pray for myself and for others so we will all be overcomers.

On the back cover of this book is a picture of me holding one of our chickens. On our hobby farm, we have three young Isa Brown chickens and one older California Gray. They illustrate how people's relationships can be with God. The old, Gray chicken won't come near me. She's way too proud, and too busy bossing the other chickens around. At nightfall, we lock up the young chickens in a coop to protect them from wild animals. They appreciate this and do not resist. When they see me get out of the car, they come running to greet me. As I turn toward them, they crouch down with lowered heads waiting for me to pick them up and lavish my love on them. That's how I want to be as well. I want to come running to my Savior and humble myself before Him so He can pick me up and lavish me with His love. It pleases Him when we draw near to Him. We also find our true joy in this. I don't want to be like the older Gray chicken too afraid or too proud to be picked up by the one who cares for her.

I reflected upon this once in my journal.

Whether it's stormy weather or a beautiful sunny day, I want to run to You, Daddy. I just love being held in your arms close to your heart.

Suddenly the old hymn, "Just a Closer Walk With Thee" came to mind. This is my prayer too:

"Grant it, Jesus, is my plea. Daily (may we be) walking close to thee. Let it be, dear Lord, let it be."

May we all admit as Matt Maher does in his song, "Lord, I Need You," that we need Jesus every day, every hour, every minute of our lives. For those who put their faith and trust in Him, He will defend. He will lead them onto paths of righteousness, and He will guide their hearts.

7

Write Your

Story

"Who shall separate us from the love of Christ? Shall trouble or hardship or persecution or famine or nakedness or danger or sword? No, in all these things we are more than conquerors through Him who loved us. For I am convinced that neither death nor life, neither angels nor demons, neither the present nor the future, nor any powers, neither height nor depth, nor anything else in all creation, will be able to separate us from the love of God that is in Christ Jesus our Lord." (Romans 8:35, 37-39)

Dear Daddy,

Thank You for the opportunity to go to church, Your house of worship, to praise You and to continue growing in my faith. In his sermon, Pastor Dave reminded us that You are not an "On-Demand God." If I pray for something and You do not answer the way I want or think You should, help me to realize this is Your story, not mine. You are not here to serve me. I am here to serve You. Your heart is always loving. God, Your ways are always higher! In times when I do not understand why something has happened – help me continue to know that You are good, loving, powerful, and in control. Let me trust You. You are God and I am not! As You remind me in Isaiah 55:8-9: "My thoughts are not your thoughts, neither are your ways My ways. As the heavens are higher than the earth, so are My ways higher than your ways and My thoughts than your thoughts." You have not given up on us or forgotten us. You are there with us through the storms. You are at work and we can see Your hand in all things. God, Your presence is always enough for me. You are my Rock! You are for me not against me! You are always there! When I read Psalm 23:4, I am convinced that I must not be afraid! Your presence is enough, even in the darkest times.

God, I ask that You always remind me that You are there, even if I question it. Let me be still and know that You are God – You will be exalted among the nations! You will be exalted in the earth (based on Psalm 46:10). This is Your show!

My spirit sings with the group, Kutless, in "Even If." Let me hold on to who You really are. Let me trust You, God. You are good. You are faithful, the great and Mighty One. You work all things for our good.

I will praise You! Even when the healing does not come.

As I was writing this book, I prayed that my words would reflect what God wanted me to say. Since I prayed over this a lot, I carefully chose the words that I would write. Misleading people is the last thing I want to do. I just want to speak the truth with love. I also didn't want to reveal things that God does not want me to reveal. Jesus promised as written in Matthew 18:20: "For where two or three are gathered in My name, there I am with them." For these reasons, I relied not only on my own thinking, but also on the great advice from my wonderful writing coaches. I wish I had a team with me all the time to filter my speech, but I know, when I lean more on the Holy Spirit, He will guide me.

God's not done writing my story, or yours, but I believe He wants us to testify of the great things He has done for us. This is what brings glory to God's great name. I also believe this is one of the ways that one man sharpens another man (Proverbs 27:17). We were not there when Jesus was raised from the dead. We were not eyewitnesses. Our testimony, however, is how we have seen Him at work in our own lives. This reminds me of Francesca Battistelli's song, "Write Your Story." I hope you pray this prayer with me.

Dear Daddy,

I want You to show this world all that You have done for me. When my writing days are almost over, I want to be able to say, "Lord, only You have written my story."

God answered my prayers and helped my prayer life become more like that of the older woman I admired in the movie "_War Room_."[1] Someone once said, "Don't I wish I was retired like you, Sheryl. I don't have time to sit and write for endless hours." What I answered to that is to just do what the Spirit prompts you to do. He may not be asking you to do that. Maybe it's only twelve minutes in the morning while you're having your coffee or tea. Pastor Dave said in a sermon one time that there was a study that showed measurable changes in your brain that can take place when you spend twelve minutes a day for eight weeks intentionally praying.[2] This may be what Paul was referring to as the renewing of our minds in Romans 12:2. For example, when you're in your car and listening to the radio your heart can suddenly be touched by the words of a Christian song or a preacher.

It may be good to write down what God was saying to you when you arrive at your destination, even if it's just on your smart phone. Maybe you often take the train to work, then instead of playing games on your phone, it may be good to read and study the Bible or talk about God with the people around you. You could also take a look at your notes from last Sunday's sermon. Maybe you often talk about God with your friends at church. When you get back home, you can further meditate on that. Whatever you do, what's really important is that you're thinking about what God may be saying to you with an open, humble heart, a heart that is willing to listen and do what God says.

Someday, when prayer journaling, you may want to consider putting in an index. This will help you find topics. It sure helped me when writing this book and sometimes when I want to share something with a friend.

Here is an example of how to create an index:

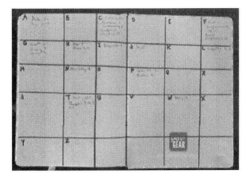

- Go back two pages from the end of your journal.

- Divide the pages so you have at least 24 sections. There are different ways you can do this depending on your style of journal. One way I found is like the one pictured. Another way I've done this is by dividing the page into seven columns by drawing six lines across (a ruler is useful). Then draw a vertical line down the middle of each index page.

- Label each section with a capital letter from the alphabet in order (You can put x, y, and z in one section).

- If your journal does not have page numbers, number each page until you get to the index.

- Right after I have written in my journal, I think about what the topic or main theme of what I had written was. That word I label by writing it down together with the page number in the right section in the index. For example, "forgiveness" belongs to section "F." This is how I quickly find topics in my journals.

  I also put a number one on the inside cover of my first journal, and for each consecutive journal, I wrote what book number it is, so my second book was labeled 2, etc. I do this because I found it interesting to go back and see my journals in the order I had written them.

Whether you prayer journal or not, I hope you let God write His story on your heart. I pray you sing along with Francesca Battistelli and me in "Write Your Story." My prayer for you is that you will come to God as an empty page and an open book in which He may write His story.

8

Jesus, Friend of Sinners

"What shall we conclude then? Do we have any advantage? Not at all! For we have already made the charge that Jews and Gentiles alike are all under the power of sin." (Romans 3:9)

Because of Adam's sin, no one is immune to death.[1] Since "everyone who calls on the Name of the Lord will be saved," according to Romans 10:13, people who have never heard the gospel are in desperate need to have it preached to them.[2] For "faith comes from hearing the message, and the message is heard through the word about Christ." (Romans 10:17)

Dear Daddy,

I know that you don't have to go outside the country to find people that are still in need of Your gospel message. There are many. I used to think that we have so many churches around Western Michigan that people must have already heard the message by now or just don't want to hear it. After all, I figured, anyone is welcome to go and hear it. Then I met someone at my church who has made me aware of how wrong that thinking was. She did not know, until someone told her. She did not attend a church to find out. If you think about it, we all lived as God's enemies, but Jesus came to us so that we could know Him as our Savior. He sent His disciples out into the world to make disciples.

I'm so glad someone shared the gospel with this friend of mine! Her love and enthusiasm for the Lord has inspired me. How many more people are out there to whom the gospel was never preached? You have made me realize how important it is to share Your message with others and to understand that we are all in need of Your saving grace. You make me want to share Your "Good News" like the singer Mandisa.

You may be questioning why I decided to donate the proceeds from this book to the missionaries in Belgium and not to the Hondurans. I will have to admit, that's a hard one for me. Although the people in Honduras will still have my support, my heart still went out to Belgium. The story below explains why.

On the morning of my departure from Belgium, I prayed, *"If You seat me next to someone who likes to talk, I will talk to them about You."* God did just that on my connecting flight from Denmark. After a little general conversation, I asked the nice gentleman if he was a Christian. He asked, "What's a Christian?"

That just threw me for a loop for a bit, but I thought, "Well, maybe it's just a language barrier." I quickly responded, "It's someone who believes in Jesus." (I should have added, "and have gladly received Him as their resurrected Lord and Savior.")

He replied that he is Lutheran, and his wife is Catholic. Yes, he believes in Jesus and that Jesus was a good man who showed us how to live. He further explained that he didn't believe in God or eternal life. "Wow," I said, "Then you have no hope."

"No," he reflected, "I guess I'm doomed."

"I think so," I said quietly, "but I hope not." My heart broke for this man sitting beside me, and I silently prayed that the Father would open his eyes.

After a few minutes, he asked me what I believe. I told him that I believe Jesus is who He said

He was, the Son of God. I explained to him that He died for us sinners and was raised from the dead to show that He truly was, and is, who He claimed to be. If He was only a good teacher, then His words would have been void. C.S. Lewis, a known British writer, explained this idea as follows: "A man who was merely a man and said the sort of things Jesus said would not be a great moral teacher. He would either be a lunatic – on a level with the man who says he is a poached egg – or else he would be the Devil of Hell. You must make your choice. Either this man was, and is, the Son of God: or else a madman or something worse . . . . You can shut Him up for a fool, you can spit at Him and kill Him as a demon; or you can fall at His feet and call Him Lord and God. But let us not come up with any patronizing nonsense about His being a great human teacher. He has not left that open to us. He did not intend to."[3]

My neighbor asked if that's what other Christians believe in America. I told him that I couldn't speak for all of America, but I know that there are many people in Western Michigan that believe that way. He even knew he was heading to the "Bible Belt" of

America, Tennessee. I prayed that he would meet some believers there.

Furthermore, I suggested He watch the YouTube video called "Man or Rabbit" by C.S. Lewis.[4] I told him that C.S. Lewis was an atheist who eventual realized that faith was reasonable because he had looked at all the evidence. At last, I told the gentleman, that doubting God's existence is normal, but that he may want to look at all of the evidence before concluding that God does not exist.

Nevertheless, people can have all the evidence in the world and witness great miracles, and yet never have saving faith. Eventually it all comes down to admitting we are a sinner in need of a Savior. In order to be reconciled to God, we must accept God's love and salvation plan. Yes, God Almighty exists, AND He loves us. He wants a relationship with us! How AMAZING is that!

I believe God has used this experience to open my eyes to the great spiritual need in Western Europe. This encounter confirmed that what William and the other Christians in Belgium had been saying to me was true. God gave me the desire to dedicate this book to them. Therefore, it's my wish that the proceeds of this book go to the ministry of William and Lyssa.

I was lost, but Jesus died for sinners just like me. Out of gratefulness and repentance, I fall down at His feet. He is good and His love endures forever! He has opened my eyes to the need in this world. "They just need to make Jesus LORD of their lives," I used to say. But God, in His mercy, has humbled me to know that it is not just them, but me as well. He has broken my heart to what breaks His and has helped me to speak His truth with love and grace and not point fingers.

I am grateful to know, like the group Casting Crowns, that "Jesus, (is a) Friend of Sinners." I pray that my family, fellow Americans and people in Belgium and all over the world will also come to realize this.

My Prayer for You

I am a child of God who has tried her best to share her testimony of how God has worked in her life. I believe this is what God called me to do. If you were encouraged when reading this book, then know it is the Holy Spirit working in you. Praise be to the Lord, our God, because He works in mysterious ways that are beyond our comprehension. To Him be all glory, honor, and praise! Amen!

Why did I title the book "God Won"? I believe that Jesus was victorious at breaking the wall that separates us from God. Satan has no "right" anymore to rule over those who have accepted Jesus as their Lord and Savior. When we pray to God and meditate on His Word, the Holy Spirit opens our eyes to the truth. If we chase the truth, we can destroy the walls of deceit we have allowed Satan to build. God tears down those walls by showing us who He is, who we are in Him, and how much we need Him. In place of the walls of deceit, God builds walls of protection, so that I do not need to fear Satan's lies and attacks. I can stand firm and trust in God as my stronghold. The crazy thing is that through total surrender, I became an overcomer.

Dear Daddy,

Whether my friends choose to journal or not, I pray that they will surrender their heart, mind and will to You and let You tear down any walls of deceit they may have. Daddy, please give them the courage and desire to share Your great love with others. Please let them know that Alisa Turner's song, "My Prayer for You" is my prayer for them as well.

In Jesus' Name, Amen.

Acknowledgments

This book would not be possible This book would not be possible without the assistance and encouragement of a great team. I would like to offer a heartfelt thank you to:

William Bode – What an unexpected vision you gave me for writing a chapter book. Thank you for giving me encouragement and suggestions along the way for the rearrangement of chapters and adding a verse and a prayer at the beginning of each chapter.

Rodney Crane – How I delight in having you for my husband. Thank you for the countless hours listening to me read this book to you and for your valuable input. I am truly grateful for your understanding of my middle of the night writing rendezvous with Jesus. Your love for me is a mirror of Christ's love for the Church. I genuinely appreciate who you are in Him.

ACKNOWLEDGMENTS

David Hansen – Your careful review of this document gave me great assurance. I know that you are a man after God's own heart and would speak the truth if something were not true about the theology in this book.

Sara Hansen – You gave me a whole new outlook for structure and transitions of my paragraphs. I thought you'd just be checking for sentence structure, spelling and punctuation, but you gave me so much more.

Delia King – It has been such a joy to work with you, my beloved sister-in-law. Thank you for asking such good questions and for your many suggestions which helped make my writing sound smooth and clear. Because of the way I first thought I heard God speaking to me through songs, your suggestion of having the titles of songs as chapter headers touched my heart.

Dorothy Mercer – You took my text and made it look like a book. I am grateful to you for your loving labor on layout.

Suzanna Monard – You are a kindred spirit. You ended up being not just a translator for the Dutch edition, but a great writing coach, fellow prayer warrior and dear friend as well.

Matt and Adrian Petree – You took my ideas for a cover design and brought them to life. Thank you for using your God-given talents to make this image a reality.

Finally – Thanks to God, who has given me the strength and will to write this book. He promises us in Philippians 4:19 that He will supply all our needs according to His riches in glory in Christ Jesus, and this is what He has also done while writing this book. He sent the right people to help me. To God be the glory both now and forever.

GOD WON

Notes

Introduction

1. Meyers, K. (2018). Grown-Up Faith: The Big Picture for a Bigger Life. In K. Meyers, *Grown-Up Faith: The Big Picture for a Bigger Life.* Nashville: Leadership Gravit, LLC, and Wetzel & Wetzel, LLC.
2. Meyers, K. (2018). Grown-Up Faith: The Big Picture for a Bigger Life. In K. Meyers, *Grown-Up Faith: The Big Picture for a Bigger Life.* Nashville: Leadership Gravit, LLC, and Wetzel & Wetzel, LLC.
3. Meyers, K. (2018). Grown-Up Faith: The Big Picture for a Bigger Life. In K. Meyers, *Grown-Up Faith: The Big Picture for a Bigger Life* (p. 195). Nashville: Leadership Gravit, LLC, and Wetzel & Wetzel, LLC.
4. Romans 8:15.

Chapter 1: As We Seek Your Face

1. Storm, S. (2017, September 29). *10 Things You Should Know about Christian Meditation.* Retrieved from Crosswalk.com: https://www.crosswalk.com/faith/spiritual-life/10-things-you-should-know-about-christian-meditation.html
2. Acts 20:28-31.

3. Romans 8:28.
4. Philippians 4:19.
5. Revelation 5:6-12.

Chapter 2: Who Am I?

1. Spurgeon, C. (1859, January 16). *C.H. Spurgeon :: Jacob and Esau.* Retrieved from blueletterbible: http://www.blueletterbible.org/Comm/spurgeon charles/sermons/0239.cfm
2. Stephen Kendrick, G. W. (Producer), & Kendrick, A. (Director). (2015). *War Room* [Motion Picture].
3. Psalm 118:8; Jeremiah 17:5-12; Hebrews 4:15; Philippians 2:5-8; Matthew 7:24-27.
4. 1 Thessalonians 5:12-22.
5. 1 Peter 5:8.
6. Isaiah 64:6.
7. Groeschel, C. (2018, September 14). *When You Believe in God but Are Ashamed of Your Past.* Retrieved from faithgateway: https://www.faithgateway.com/believe-god-ashamed-past/#.XdGRgSVOnYU
8. Groeschel, C. (2018, September 14). *When You Believe in God but Are Ashamed of Your Past.* Retrieved from faithgateway: https://www.faithgateway.com/believe-god-ashamed-past/#.XdGRgSVOnYU
9. Groeschel, C. (2018, September 14). *When You Believe in God but Are Ashamed of Your Past.* Retrieved from faithgateway: https://www.faithgateway.com/b

elieve-god-ashamed-
past/#.XdGRgSVOnYU
10. Groeschel, C. (2018, September
14). *When You Believe in God but Are
Ashamed of Your Past.* Retrieved
from faithgateway:
https://www.faithgateway.com/b
elieve-god-ashamed-
past/#.XdGRgSVOnYU
11. Groeschel, C. (2018, September
14). *When You Believe in God but Are
Ashamed of Your Past.* Retrieved
from faithgateway:
https://www.faithgateway.com/b
elieve-god-ashamed-
past/#.XdGRgSVOnYU
12. 12.   Romans 8:28.
13. Matthew 18:12.

Chapter 3: Reckless Love

1. McAllister, D. (n.d.). *Why Did God
Create Us: He doesn't really need us, so
why did he create anything?* Retrieved
from ignite your faith:
https://christianitytoday.com/iyf
/advice/faithdoubt/why-did-god-
create-man.html
2. Genesis 1:26.
3. 1 John 4:8.
4. Deuteronomy 6:5.
5. Matthew 22:39.
6. Ephesians 2:10.
7. Ephesians 6:10-18.
8. 2 Corinthians 5:18-20.

Chapter 4: Open the Eyes of My

Heart, Lord

NOTES

1. Stephen Kendrick, G. W. (Producer), & Kendrick, A. (Director). (2015). *War Room* [Motion Picture].
2. Chan, F. (2013). Crazy Love. In F. Chan, *Crazy Love: Overwhelmed by a Relentless God*. Colorado Springs: David C Cook.
3. Chan, F. (2013). Crazy Love. In F. Chan, *Crazy Love: Overwhelmed by a Relentless God. (Chapter 2)*. Colorado Springs: David C Cook.
4. Joshua 1:9.
5. 1 Corinthians 12:27.
6. 1 Corinthians 15:58.
7. 1 Corinthians 12:14.
8. Daniel 7:27; Romans 8:16-17; Revelation 22:5.

Chapter 5: God is on the Move

1. Haworth, E. (2020, September 18). *The three elements of salvation*. Retrieved from Knowing-Jesus: https://devotion.knowing-jesus.com/the-three-elements-of-salvation#:~:text=%20The%20Three%20Elements%20of%20Salvation%20%201,were%20saved%20at%20a%20single%20point...%20More%20
2. Redpath, D. A. (1961). *A call to consecration*. Retrieved from My Church Media: https://www.moodymedia.org/articles/call-consecration/
3. Haworth, E. (2020, September 18). *The three elements of salvation*. Retrieved from Knowing-Jesus: https://devotion.knowing-jesus.com/the-three-elements-of-salvation#:~:text=%20The%20T

hree%20Elements%20of%20Salv
ation%20%201,were%20saved%2
0at%20a%20single%20point...%2
0More%20

4. 1 John 3:2.

5. Wommack, A. (2021). *Eternal life
   there's more to it than you think.*
   Retrieved from Andrew
   Wommack Ministries:
   https://www.awmi.net/reading/t
   eaching-articles/eternal_life/

6. Romans 8:29.
7. Isaiah 45:5.
8. 1 Thessalonians 1:10.
9. Luke 2:11.
10. John 8:12.
11. 1 John 1:7.
12. James 4:8.
13. James 4:5-10.
14. Malachi 1:6.
15. Stucki, J. (2016, July 26). *Two
    Common Misuses of God's Name.*
    Retrieved from Unlocking the
    Bible:
    http://unlockingthebible.org/201
    6/07/two-common-misuses-of-
    gods-name/
16. Deuteronomy 18:20, 22.
17. Philippians 1:6.
18. Ephesians 5:23.
19. Proverbs 21:19.
20. 1 Peter 5:7, emphasis added.
21. Weizhou Tang, K.K. (2017, July).
    *Archives of gerontology and geriatrics:
    Concern about developing Alzheimer's
    disease or dementia and intention to be
    screened: An analysis of national survey
    data.* Retrieved from
    Ncbi.nlm.nih.gov:

https://pubmed.ncbi.nlm.nih.gov
/28279898/
22. An, J.H., Lee, K.E., Jeon, H.J. *et al.*
Risk of suicide and accidental
deaths among elderly patients with
cognitive impairments. *Alz Res
Therapy* **11**, 32 (2019).
https://doi.org/10.1186/s13195-
019-0488-x
23. 1 Corinthians 6:20.
24. John 10:10.

Chapter 6: Lord, I Need You

1. Sacks, O. (Writer), & Marshall, P.
(Director). (1990). *Awakenings*
[Motion Picture].
2. Vogel, J. (1990). *Awakenings Plot.*
Retrieved from IMDb:
https://www.imdb.com/title/tt00
99077/plotsummary
3. Matthew 4:6.
4. Exodus 14.
5. 1 John 3:1.
6. Isaiah 59:2.
7. The Bible Project. (2018, March
15). *Word Study: Khata - Sin.*
Retrieved from YouTube:
https://www.bing.com/videos/se
arch?q=(https%3a%2f%2fm.yout
ube.com%2fwatch%3fv%3danoz
7ocld74&view=detail&mid=8D1
1A2851EB5654E09888D11A285
1EB5654E0988&FORM=VIRE
8. The Bible Project. (2018, March
15). *Word Study: Khata - Sin.*
Retrieved from YouTube:
https://www.bing.com/videos/se
arch?q=(https%3a%2f%2fm.yout
ube.com%2fwatch%3fv%3danoz
7ocld74&view=detail&mid=8D1

1A2851EB5654E09888D11A285
1EB5654E0988&FORM=VIRE

9. Meyers, K. (2018). Grown-Up Faith: The Big Picture for a Bigger Life. In K. Meyers, *Grown-Up Faith: The Big Picture for a Bigger Life* (p. 195). Nashville: Leadership Gravit, LLC, and Wetzel & Wetzel, LLC.

10. Philippians 3:14.

11. Devos Archives. (2019, March 10). *God Forgives Only the Broken and Contrite Heart.* Retrieved from Kids 4 Truth Clubs Equip U Online Library: Free Children's Ministry Resources: https://equipu.kids4truth.com/god-forgives-only-the-broken-and-contrite-heart/

12. Devos Archives. (2019, March 10). *God Forgives Only the Broken and Contrite Heart.* Retrieved from Kids 4 Truth Clubs Equip U Online Library: Free Children's Ministry Resources: https://equipu.kids4truth.com/god-forgives-only-the-broken-and-contrite-heart/

13. John 17:6.

14. John 10:10.

15. Revelation 12:9.

16. 1 John 2:1-2 .

17. Philippians 2:13.

Chapter 7: Write Your Story

1. Stephen Kendrick, G. W. (Producer), & Kendrick, A. (Director). (2015). *War Room* [Motion Picture].

2. Hayes, C. (2016, November 18). *How Prayer Changes Your Brain*

Structure. Retrieved from Grow the Heck Up: http://growtheheckup.com/how-prayer-changes-your-brain-structure

Chapter 8: Jesus, Friend of Sinners

1. Romans 5:12.
2. Romans 10:14.
3. Lewis, C. (1952). *Mere Christianity.* Geoffrey Bles.
4. Lewis, C. (2014, May 12). *Man or Rabbit.* Retrieved from YouTube: https://www.bing.com/videos/search?q=man+or+rabbit+youtube&view=detail&mid=BF41AB2926C6785597E9BF41AB2926C6785597E9&FORM=VIRE

Made in the USA
Middletown, DE
15 May 2022